WOMEN AND INFORMATION TECHNOLOGY

Ongoing Challenges for Computing and Information Technology Education

WOMEN AND INFORMATION TECHNOLOGY

Ongoing Challenges for Computing and Information Technology Education

Asha Srivastava

MD PUBLICATIONS PVT LTD
NEW DELHI
www.mdppl.com

Published by :

MD Publications Pvt Ltd
"MD House", 11, Darya Ganj,
New Delhi - 110 002
Phone : +91-11-45355555
E-mail : contact@mdppl.com
Website: www.mdppl.com

ISBN: 978-81-7533-252-2

Published and Printed by Mr. Pranav Gupta on behalf of **MD Publications Pvt Ltd** at Mohit Enterprises, Delhi.

PREFACE

Women have been involved in computers since computers were first envisioned. They are present in all facets of computing and information technology. Despite this, their presence is comparatively small in these fields, and the fact of their overall under representation has been established. A proposal from an economical standpoint suggests that in order to avert the computing and IT industry from dangers such as global sourcing, a solution is needed to increase the participation of underrepresented groups like women.

The Information Technology field has steadily increased in importance over the course of many years. The field of IT has also been traditionally controlled and advanced by men. In the last few years, perhaps due to the increasing salary benefits, more and more women are embracing the world of IT. As with any field not used to an influx of the female gender, there are some growing pains. Women often face problems with sexual harassment; suffer from a general lack of faith in their technical abilities; and are often kept out of the loop.

Sexual harassment happens in nearly every environment and thus is not unique to women in IT. There may be a difference only in that in a higher paying industry that is so dominantly ruled by men, the incentive to keep quiet is stronger. Women take these IT jobs for the same reasons as men such as financial rewards, advancement, education, and pure enjoyment. Despite the growing number of women online, the content and culture of the internet remain male-dominated. Young women exploring the internet often encounter hateful material, violence, sexism, homophobia, racism, pornography, etc., which may cause discomfort and make the internet an unwelcome place for some.

Women face a variety of obstacles when entering this high tech and competitive industry. It is just key to remember that whether the problem is sexual harassment, lack of respect, or trouble breaking into the "boys club" that the benefits far outweigh the cost. High salaries and respect are a payoff that comes from a job in Information Technology, a far cry from the days of a woman's duty to be a secretary or receptionist. Having self-confidence enough in ones own abilities and finding the balance of respect and understanding can avoid all three of these taboo issues.

I am very grateful to Mr. Pranav Gupta, Director of MD Publications Pvt Ltd, New Delhi, for his kind cooperation and support for this book.

Asha Srivastava

CONTENTS

CONTENTS

1

Technological Rationality in the Human Sciences

There is no need to emphasize for this audience that the fundamental project of technology threatens to create a vast necropolis for the earth. Dangerously close is the realization of the ancient prophetic warning of a Hindu sacred scripture which says: "I am my death." In this chapter, the central concern is with technology's potential to destroy the philosophy of the social sciences. What is offered is a critique of technological rationality. Most important, it is argued that all the calculative or technological models of cognition are incapable of rendering sociality-the most fundamental concept of the social sciences-as discourse between the self and the other.

The basis of this contention is that technological rationality overlooks and is incapable of understanding the body as the active and synergistic mode of existing in the world. If, as Maurice Merleau-Ponty contends, all science outlines ontology, then it is possible to fathom reality as social. This suggests not simply that social existence is constructed but, more fundamentally, reality is tied intimately to the human presence.

By genealogy is meant a critical analysis of genesis, or meaning genesis, the quintessence of phenomenological thinking. To paraphrase Merleau-Ponty in order to accent this genealogical spirit: The end of the phenomenological philosophy is the account of its beginning. In essence, the true phenomenologist is necessarily and always a perpetual beginner in the search for meaning. But before phenomenologists such as Edmund Husserl, Martin Heidegger, and Merleau-Ponty, Friedrich Nietzsche pioneered genealogy as a mode of philosophical inquiry based on the aesthetics of music.

In Nietzsche's genealogy there is the ineluctable enmeshing of origin and value; that is, the reversibility of the value of origin and the origin of value that implies the eternal re-turning of values. Genealogy purports to break the iron grip of established reality and demands a rediscovery of existence that cannot be extricated from values. Accordingly, genealogy is both destructive and constructive at the same time. In *The Basic Problems of Phenomenology*, Heidegger suggests that deconstruction reduces traditional concepts to the source from which they originate, while reestablishing them on the value base illustrated by this process.

As mentioned earlier, sociality may be defined as the discourse, or diatactics, of the self and other. The neologism diatactics is coined by Hayden White as a replacement for the term dialectics, in order to avoid any association with Karl Marx or Georg Hegel. As applied to sociality, diatactics is neither overdetermination nor underdetermination of the self by the other. Sociality may be said to have two sides: for example, sociability and asociability, cooperation and conflict, and war and peace. For the purpose of this chapter, the term *diatactics* is appropriated in two additional ways.

In the first place, the logic of diatactics connotes historical movement or change without any teleological progression. For Jose Ortegay Gasset this is the essence of "historical reason": "If I say that something is *movement*, I am saying it is A but that it is also B, for it has changed." Hence, diatactics is embedded in the sense of ambiguity. For the *etyma "ambi-"* means "bothness" as in ambivalence and "aroundness" as in ambiance. Ambiance, milieu, circumstance, and environment are all familial or neighboring concepts. Sociality is therefore a diatactical complicity of distinction and equality. Equality suggests that a common ground exists so as to allow for communication among persons.

Yet if humans were not distinct, there would again be no need to communicate. Distinction-individual differences-is essential for human plurality, as individualism assumes a radical alterity of the other person. Again, there are many different languages in the history of human civilization. Not only is each way of speaking distinct, as each individual appropriates language somewhat uniquely, all communication of understanding within a linguistic system is a sort of translation among persons. In this sense, identity and difference exist together.

In the second place, diatactics implies sense perception or the sensorium. More specifically, it arouses not only the intimate sense of touch, insofar as it is tactical, but also the synesthesia or synergy of the entire sensorium necessary to organize perception. As it rejects the dualist approach to mind and body, diatactics incorporates conception with perception, for there is no rationality that is not intimately associated with human actions. Merleau-Ponty insists that as consciousness is to the body, so the "I think" (*cogito*) is to the "I perceive" (*percipio*).

His emphasis on corporeality, or the body, as the subject of perception is an urge to return to perception that is always tainted by a person's existential condition. Thus, he insists that perception is a nascent way of translating the world. Perception, in short, is not merely a passive process whereby knowledge is received but rather gives form to what is known. Yet most often perception is viewed undiatactically, or dualistically. Nonetheless, the separation of interpretation and perception, as well as that of mind and body, is artificial. An examination of the work of Rene Descartes is thus central to a diatactical understanding of sociality.

DESCARTES AND THE MODERN WORLD

Since genealogy implies genesis, meaning genesis, the modern origin of technological rationality can be traced to Descartes. For him, certainty resides in a conceptualization of philosophy as *mathesis universalis*. Descartes is solidifying the view of Galileo, who wrote in *Il Saggiatore* that "Philosophy written in that vast book which stands forever open before our eyes, I mean the universe; but it cannot be read until we have learned the language and become familiar with the characters in which it is written. It is written in mathematical language, and the letters are triangles, circles, and other geometrical figures, without which means it is humanly impossible to comprehend a single word." The mathematical measuring of the universe, however, is nothing new; it goes back to Pythagoras and his followers-including Plato-in ancient Greece.

What is new with the modern conception of mathematics, however, is that it attends first and last to method, whereas the ancients addressed the problem of method in terms of more fundamental philosophical questions. Jacob Klein argues that in modern science the "generality of the method" (methodology) replaced the "generality of the object" (ontology). Descartes also set in motion the idea that clear thinking could only be guaranteed through the use of mathematics. Thus, quantification became the road to truth.

Moreover, philosophical certainty, for Descartes, results from the mind being a "thinking substance" (*res cogitans*). However valid or invalid the analogy of "a pilot in a vessel" may be, there is a problem with characterizing the mind as a thinking substance, because as a substance it needs nothing more than itself to exist. That is to say, insofar as the mind is not *indigens* it must be independent of the body as well as of other minds. If there is a union between mind and body it is a weak or loose one. The problem with the Cartesian *cogito*, or the mind, as the basis of explaining sociality is at least threefold.

First, the *cogito* is inherently egocentric because it is always and necessarily *ego cogito* (the "I think"), or the epitome of an "inner man" in isolation from others. Second, to say that mind is a thinking substance (*res*), following the Greek and Scholastic traditions, is to say that it needs nothing more than itself to exist. Once the self and the other are viewed as substances, which is to say two separate substances, egocentrism or even solipsism is inevitable. Third, and most importantly, sociality is not merely a meeting of minds, disembodied minds alone, but is first and foremost intercorporeal. The seminal contribution of phenomenology to the human or behavioural sciences is the notion of embodiment, whose basic thesis is that the body is not an object but is primarily a subject.

The body is not an object to be had in the sense of a possession, but is an active mode of existing in the world. "I *am* my body," declares Gabriel Marcel, "in so far as I succeed in recognizing that this body of mine *cannot*, in the last analysis, be brought down to the level of being this object, *an* object, a something or other. It is at this point that we have to bring in the idea of the body not as an object but as a subject." This phenomenological notion of the body rejects the Cartesian analogy of mind and body as "a pilot in a vessel." Since it is neither purely materiality nor spirituality, the body is capable of acting as a hinge between the self and the other. In essence, the body inhabits the world. Because of this, the body is both aware of itself and its limits and therefore is open to the other.

This means that social order can be engendered directly among persons, or intercorporeally. Nonetheless, Descartes nullifies this possibility, as he imagines the self to be a thing. For Descartes, thinking is a matter arriving at clear and distinct ideas. Philosophy, as a *mathesis universalis*, is thoroughly compatible with a visual metaphysics. For him, clarity means that objects are present to the mind's eye without being mistaken about their qualities. The idea of distinction simply enhances the notion of clarity, in that an object must be well defined and different from other objects. Therefore, Cartesian metaphysics based on the *cogito* understands vision to be unambiguous, particularly if all perceptual apparatuses are working properly.

As a matter of fact, visual metaphysics goes hand in hand with the egocentrism of the *cogito*. For it has been shown that, unlike the other forms of the human sensorium (for example, hearing), vision denies the sociability of the senses. Sound tends to socialize, unify, and synthesize, whereas sight tends to isolate, divide, and analyze. In other words, there is an identity, or isomorphism, between the "eye" and the "I." As vision demotes the other senses, so does the *cogito* overlook and theorize away the other person. Heidegger maintains that the I (or the eye) of the Cartesian *cogito* becomes the center of thought, from which the "I-viewpoint," or egoism, of modern thought originates.

In this Cartesian proposition, the one who posits and thinks is the I of the *cogito*: "the subjectivity of the subject is determined by the 'I-ness' (*Ichheit*) of the 'I think.'" For Heidegger, in other words, the I-viewpoint of the Cartesian cogito coincides with the modern age. Visual metaphysics and egoism are one and the same process and are central to solving the problems associated with technological rationality in the modern world. Particularly, subverting Descartes' visual metaphysic is vital to placing technology in the service of the human condition.

CARTESIAN-BASED SOCIAL THEORIES

In this section, Ortega's philosophy of human existence will be used as the basis of a critique of the contemporary theories of human behaviour that reflect Cartesianism: they are B. F. Skinner's behaviourism, Edward O. Wilson's sociobiology, Herbert A. Simon's "sciences of the artificial," and Marshall McLuhan's media as autonomous technology. In one way or the other, they all "overdetermine" the self by the environment. The reason for adopting Ortega's model is threefold. First, Ortega recognized the Cartesian principle of clear and distinct ideas and the philosophical harbinger of modern technological rationality, which is grounded in the notion of purging knowledge acquisition of passion.

Second, Ortega formulation in *Meditations on Quixote* (1914) of reality as the duplexity of the I and circumstance(s) (*circumstantia*) not only antedated Heidegger's formulation of human reality (*Dasein*) as Being-in-the-world (*in-derWelt-sein*) and Husserl's formulation of the life-world (*lebenswelt*) as sociocultural reality, but also anticipated Merleau-Ponty's phenomenology of perception which rejects the dichotomization of *res cogitans (pour-soi)* and *res extensa (ensoi)*. For Ortega, reality is the diatactical correlation of the I and circumstances. He rejects the Cartesian formulation of the *cogito*, which reduces the world to the I or makes the I independent of the world. Ortega writes: "The realism of antiquity held that the reality of the world was independent of human thought.

Modern idealism holds that thought is independent of the world. I say: an *independent world or independent thought* do [*sic*] not exist." Reality, in other words, is the diatactics of the I and circumstance. Third, Ortega's formulation of circumstance is related to the English term environment. There are three kinds of environment: social, natural (both physical and biological), and technological or artificial. In terms of explanatory models of human behaviour, they correspond to the theories advanced by Skinner, Wilson, Simon, and McLuhan. Moreover, these models share something in common: the overdetermination of the self by the environment. Ortega's conception of circumstance prevents this because it is inextricably united with human creativity.

It is no accident that, in *Beyond Freedom and Dignity*, Skinner points to Descartes as the first who envisioned that the environment might play an active role in shaping human behaviour. Skinner contends that the "technology of behaviour" is important for remedying today's and tomorrow's social problems. The science of man, according to Skinner, covers two basic areas: genetic endowments and environment. He relegates the areas to biology and psychology, respectively. The boundary between the two disciplines, however, is crossed when Skinner declares without equivocation: "The environment not only prods or lashes, it *selects*. Its role is similar to that in natural selection, though on a very different time scale, and was overlooked for the same reason.

It is now clear that we must take into account what the environment does to an organism not only before but after it responds. Behaviour is shaped and maintained by its consequences." He cringes at the hint of "mentalism" (the mind as an autonomous substance), "uncaused" behaviour, or an inner man (*homunculus*). For Skinner there is no autonomous man. Instead, he offers a thoroughgoing determination of the self by the environment. Skinner even rejects the explanatory model based on information theory or cybernetics because it is predicated on the existence of an "inner processor." He insists, therefore, that his science of human behaviour does not represent an attempt to dehumanize but only to "dehomunculize" persons.

The genesis of this environmentalism in Skinner can be traced most clearly to Descartes theory of music in *Abrege de la Musique*, which was written under the influence of Marin Mersenne. Descartes was driven to examine all objects, including aesthetic objects, with the attitude that certitude is demonstrable in geometric theorems. Music, too, is likened to mathematics. In his theory of music, as in philosophy, he strives for clear and distinct knowledge by controlling his passions, thereby revealing beauty. This means that the "beauty" of an aesthetic principle is as simple or elegant as arithmetic or a geometric figure. Following the mathematical theorists of his time, Descartes rationalized musical harmony in terms of mathematical equations and diagrams.

For him, mathematically induced harmony symbolizes clear and distinct thinking. Consistent with this scientific and technological rationality, what is most interesting about Descartes's view of music is his theory of sound or acoustics. For him, the object of music is sound. "For him," John Hollander writes, "the essence of music is instrumental sound, or the vocal intonation of sound modelled on the former, the voice being treated as merely another instrument. For him, in short, the effects of music upon feelings are purely matters of acoustics and physiology." With Descartes, even the human voice becomes objective or "instrumental."

Sociobiology is a combination of biology and sociology. It attempts to generalize about social behaviour from the vantage point of biology. In fact, sociobiology is envisioned as "a new human science." According to Charles J. Lumsden and Edward O. Wilson, "Defined as the study of the biological basis of social behaviour, it [sociobiology] carries evolutionary theory into the previously un-Darwinized fields of psychology and the social sciences." Sociobiology is a form of scientism that assumes that "All domains of human life, including ethics, have a physical basis in the brain and are part of human biology; none is exempt from analysis in the mode of the natural sciences." Thus, sociobiology is reductionistic in that all behaviour is explained according to biological principles.

Lumsden and Wilson admit this when they argue that sociobiology decomposes complicated systems into manageable components for scientific analysis, while also reassembling these parts so that their validity can be tested by experimentation or mathematical formulations. On the question of purpose in human behaviour, sociobiology adopts a mechanistic model and portrays moral judgment as a physiological product of the brain and as such can be simulated by computers. "Sophisticated goals," Lumsden and Wilson insist, "can be built into machines." In this respect, sociobiologist's advocate social engineering, or what Skinner calls the "technology of behaviour," to alter every part of human behaviour, including the deepest levels of human motivation and moral reasoning.

Sociobiology is Cartesian to the extent that the reality of mental phenomena (for example, thinking and moral reasoning) can be computed or calculated experimentally or mathematically in alliance with "cognitive psychology." Insofar as all mental phenomena are assumed to be products of brain physiology, the rationality of sociobiology may be likened to the Cartesian disembodied *cogito*. In this sense, it may be concluded that sociobiology is more reductionistic than Skinner's behaviourism, or technology of behaviour, because while Skinner's behaviourism stops at refuting the ghost in a machine, sociobiology not only reduces human existence to biological processes but also the biological to the operation of the brain and openly avows an alliance with cybernetics.

It would indeed be foolhardly to deny that biological conditions are necessary for shaping human behaviour, but sociobiology confuses necessary and sufficient conditions. In other words, it is reductionistic. This criticism of sociobiology becomes apparent against the backdrop supplied Ortega's notion of circumstance, which is related to the German idea of Umwelt (the surrounding world).

He acknowledges his indebtedness in formulating his conception of human existence to the German biologist Jakob von Uexkuell, who published in 1909 the book *Umwelt und Innenwelt der Tiere.* Uexkuell's work is thought to inaugurate the biological science known as ethology, which attempts to study animal behaviour in its natural habitat, rather than a laboratory, in order to avoid anthropocentric or anthropomorphic prejudices. It should be noted that for Lumsden and Wilson, sociobiology is related to ethology only insofar as both disciplines are interested in investigating how an organism adapts to its environment. Like cybernetics or the study of artificial intelligence, sociobiology provides merely a structural analysis of the biological system. Ortega's circumstance, however, is not the biological context of behaviour. The formulation of Ortega's "I am I and my circumstance" requires a radical distinction between the I and circumstance, where one is never reducible to the other.

Otherwise, he would commit the fallacy of both anthropomorphism (reducing animal behaviour to human forms) and theriomorphism (reducing human behaviour to animal forms, for example, the popular theory of the territorial imperatives). From the standpoint of biological theory, however, humans are a function of their environment, while the environment by and large determines all behaviour. Ortega, on the other hand, wishes to affirm the existential or ecstatic character of human reality. A circumstance exists for persons precisely because they are capable of interpreting and appropriating their environment. In this sense, Ortega's formulation of "I and my circumstance" is close to Heidegger's view of human reality as Being-in-the-world, in which the term in should not be likened to an object in space but an active way of creating a world. Thus, Ortega declares that humans have no nature but only history, for Man is the only being that is capable of bringing about changes. Life (or history) itself is not a factum (a substantive) but faciendum (a gerund), that is, something that has to be accomplished or made.

The rationality of artificial intelligence is at the apex of technological wisdom. Today it surpasses the original vision of its founder, Norbert Wiener. The philosophy of artificial intelligence is a matter not so much of creating "the second self"-to use the title of Sherry Turkle's recent study on the subject-as of replacing the thinking self with an artificial one. Like Descartes, researchers in artificial intelligence regard thinking as ultimately important.

Unlike Descartes, however, the *cogito* is reduced to abstraction and accordingly is bereft of a thinker or thinking aspect. Researchers in artificial intelligence respond to their critics: The idea that there must be an agent who does thinking is "a modern echo of the [Cartesian] idea that there must be a 'soul' in the pineal gland." Nonetheless, the post-Cartesianism of artificial intelligence preserves the physicalist legacy of Descartes. In essence, artificial intelligence both disembodies and despiritualizes persons, as isomorphism is thought to exist between human cognition and a machine.

In his most recent work, *Reason in Human Affairs*, Herbert A. Simon touches on an issue raised by Edward O. Wilson's sociobiology. For Simon, rationality is the way(s) an organism adapts to its environment for survival. He affirms the instrumental nature of science and technology for solving the problems of society and political institutions. As a matter of fact, he views reason itself as wholly instrumental. While rejecting the "Olympian model" of SEU (subjective expected utility) as "a beautiful object deserving a prominent place in Plato's heaven of ideas," he deems the central thesis of sociobiology compatible with the "behavioural model."

The evolutionary theory of sociobiology, in other words, is compatible with the behavioural model because both envision rationality as evolutionary adaptation. The behavioural model assumes that in the process of social and cultural evolution, human thinking and problem solving are factorable into various separate spheres for choosing alternatives for social improvement. Like the theory of biological evolution, it is anti-utopian. For Simon's behavioural model favors "weak altruism," or enlightened self-interest, as a person "sacrifice[s] fitness in the short run but receives indirect long-run rewards that more than compensate for the immediate sacrifice."

However, according to Simon, there is a radical difference between cultural and biological inheritance: The former, but not the latter, is "distinctly Lamarkian" and allows acquired traits to be transmitted. The acquisition of scientific knowledge is not only instrumental but incremental, as opposed to paradigmatic in the Kuhnian sense. Simon writes:

The teleology of the evolutionary process is of a rather peculiar sort. There is not a goal, only a process of searching and ameliorating. Searching is the end. I suggested earlier that evolution is sometimes regarded as a detailed explanation for rationality precisely because it doesn't require a detailed explanation of process; the important thing is adaptation, however the adaptation is brought about. Evolution permits one to postulate the ends without specifying the means. Now we see that the matter is really the other way around. Evolution, at least in a complex world, specifies means (the process of variation and selection) that do not lend to any predictable end. From ends without means, we have come full circle to means without ends.

Most interesting about Simon's behavioural model is that it is taxied, or piggybacked, by the "sciences of the artificial." For this reason, the cybernetic model is the apotheosis of behaviouralism. Simon's previous work, *The Sciences of the Artificial*, represents in an important way the most abstract strain of technological rationality and at the same time the highest overdetermination of the self by the environment. For him, the artificial is identical with the adaptive. In *Reason in Human Affairs*, adaptation is called "docility," which is defined as the propensity to behave in socially approved ways and to refrain from behaving in socially disapproved ways. Simon's docility is comparable to Skinner's understanding of reinforcement. Interestingly, docility is also called "programmability."

For Simon, human science is the science of the artificial. To "operationalize" human thinking it must be reduced to the formal, mathematical model of artificial intelligence. When a concept is operationalized in this manner, it is reduced to discrete bits of information, or "atomic facts." The acquisition of language, when treated in this way, is the process of artificialization. Simon thus declares that "there is no contradiction, then, between the thesis that a human being possesses, at birth, a competence for acquiring and using language and the thesis that language is the most artificial, hence also the most human of all human constructions." Here Simon grafts Noam Chomsky's "Cartesian linguistics" with the rationality of artificial intelligence.

By artificial, Simon means man-made or designed as opposed to natural. The synonyms for artificial intelligence are "complex information processing" and "the simulation of cognitive processes." He asserts that "the world we live in today is much more a man-made, or artificial, world than it is a natural world." And the significant parts of any environment are artifacts called "symbols." For Simon, two of the most important fields in the behavioural sciences are cognitive psychology and engineering design. For him, the Cartesian dualism of the inner and the outer disappears when the former is submerged in the latter or when the inner environment becomes simply a function of the outer environment.

Additionally, simulation does not require that the experimental base of thinking be understood for the mind to be known. The mind is allegedly revealed through the mathematical formulas that are invoked to predict how any "normal" person will react to a particular environment setting. Simon argues, to use his own terms, for "the disembodiment of mind." To understand and predict human actions, behaviour must be formalized into causal laws and formal rules that are unaffected by existential contingency.

For Simon, science and technology epitomize human rationality, as reason itself is nothing but instrumental. Thus, scientific knowledge is as natural as technology: He insists that the "ought" cannot be derived from the "is." Nevertheless, he is critical of the failure of the media to go beyond "the news and the fads of the present moment," beyond "the newsworthy, the sensational, and the novel." He comes to the conclusion that "TV is perhaps even a worse offender than the older media on this dimension because it can create not only a local trend, but a national or international focus of attention."

In this regard, Simon offers a stark contrast to Marshall McLuhan's euphoria concerning electronic technology (for example, television), which both ecumenicizes the senses and globalizes humankind. What is interesting about McLuhan for this discussion is twofold. First, the Cartesian saga of technological rationality has an unexpected twist in McLuhanism. Second, McLuhanism is the edifice of "autonomous technology," which means that technology is no more than *instrumentum*, or a method to further itself.

McLuhan, too, celebrates cybernation because it ensures the type of contact between humans and technology that allows for a return to the synesthetic interplay of the senses. For him, the visual metaphysics of Descartes epitomized in "clear and distinct" ideas reflects the highly visible order of typographic culture, which began with the Gutenburg revolution. Unlike Descartes, McLuhan is concerned primarily with the sensorial workings of the body and particularly with the tactility associated with electronic technology. To use his hyperbolic and flippant expression: "the electric light is pure information."

More importantly, McLuhan highlights the essence of autonomous technology in his celebrated slogan: "the medium is the message." For him, "the 'content' of a medium is like the juicy piece of meat carried by the burglar to distract the watch-dog of the mind." The content of any medium is always another medium. For example, the content of writing is the medium of speech; the content of print is the medium of the written word; and the content of the telegraph is the medium of print. In this sense, the environment prescribed by a medium defines the parameters of thought.

Paradoxically, it is the allegedly anti-Cartesian McLuhan who hints at a blind spot in Simon. Simon is ignorant of the categorical imperative of autonomous technology as the reversal of the traditional end-means continuum: Means has now become end. At this juncture, Heidegger's seminal reflection on the question of technology is important. He contends that the nature of technology has not been fully understood because persons have become functionaries. What has to be understood, Heidegger contends, is that the essence (*wesen*) of technology is no longer technological, for it is not just instrumental.

It is no longer simply a means for human activity. Technology is not viewed as the application of thought but thought itself. In brief, the traditional rationale of technology as *instrumentum* is obsolete and anachronistic. Nonetheless, this outmoded view is still offered today as a justification for technology. In so doing, technology is portrayed as morally neutral, rather than a means that has become an end in itself. Thus, the thinking that is necessary to control technology has tended to atrophy as techniques have unburdened humanity from having to engage in radical reflection. For the highest form of thought is presumed to be technical or logistical rationality.

In the beginning of this chapter it was proposed that the Cartesian *cogito* and its visual metaphysics are incapable of justifying sociality as the diatactics of the self and the other. On the one hand, the *cogito* is inherently egocentric because it incarcerates the self in the prison house of abstract thought. This is consistent with Descartes' metaphysics, which is driven by "clarity." To wit, the I viewpoint is the eye viewpoint. On the other hand, persons are also the *manipulandum* of the environment. For once the body becomes soulless; it is like an instrument, as exhibited in the way Descartes theorizes about the human voice. And because the *cogito* is disembodied it is ignorant of any relationship between the inner and the outer world.

It was Ortega who identified the genesis of technological rationality in Descartes's *cogito*, or *cogitatio*, that edifies philosophy as *mathesis universalis*. Skinner's technology of behaviour, the physicalism of Wilson's sociobiology, and Simon's behavioural or cybernetic model are all extensions of the Cartesian disembodied *cogito* with a radical difference: Disembodied thought has now been transformed into anonymous thought in artificial intelligence, as the *cogito* is not only disembodied but also bereft of the subject or agent who thinks. Yet in order to justify sociality, a conception of the body is needed that actively engages the world as I and circumstance. Both the *cogito* and artificial intelligence are, to put it another way, undiatactical because one is "unsocialized" and the other is "oversocialized."

The model of "oversocialized man" in artificial intelligence is incapable of explaining social change or human initiative. Moreover, the political importance of artificial intelligence is enormous: the birth of a mass society, or totalitarianism, in which society is a mass of anonymous individuals as manipulanda.

Merleau-Ponty jabs at the heart of artificialism when he writes: when "man really becomes the manipulandum he takes himself to be, we enter into a cultural regimen where there is neither truth nor falsity concerning man and history, into a sleep, or a nightmare, from which there is no awakening." In this sense, technological rationality becomes a substitue for human thinking and discourse, as technique specifies what is humanly possible. Technology cannot be spared this ignoble fate, however, unless the dualistic illusions accompanying Cartesianism are shattered.

THE LIFE-WORLD AND OF TECHNOLOGY

The philosopher Henryk Skolimowski raises two interesting points in a recent essay. First, he argues that a philosophy of technology is simultaneously a philosophical anthropology, because questions about the future of technology are questions about the future of civilization. Second, Skolimowski suggests that a philosophical analysis of technology that remains under the influence of the technological world-view will be one-sided and inadequate.

The problem, briefly, is that a philosophy of technology requires liberation from the prevailing technological attitude. Thus, Skolimowski states: "To comprehend the course of our civilization as influenced by science and technology we seek a perspective above the partial and partisan world view of the scientific-technological *Weltanschauung*."

However valid Skolimowski's observations may be, how is the requisite perspective "above" the scientific-technological world to be achieved? Skolimowski prescribes developing an awareness of alternative world-views through contact and familiarity with non-Western societies and cultures. But is this really enough? What is to prevent the technological *Weltanschauung* (world-view) from distorting nontechnological societies? If the technological attitude is really as pervasive and encompassing as Skolimowski contends, then how can a perspective above it be achieved in order to explicate, understand, and evaluate critically technology?

Philosophically, this problem is of no small consequence and requires for its solution a method to defuse the prejudices indigenous to the technological world-view. A plausible approach to this problem is outlined in the phenomenological writings of Edmund Husserl. Thus, this chapter will examine Husserl's phenomenology of the lifeworld, along with the methods of epoche and reduction, to see how it might provide a solution for the question, "How is a philosophy of technology possible?" In his last work, *The Crisis of European Sciences and Transcendental Phenomenology*, Husserl confronts a more encompassing version of the problem raised by Skolimowski. In Husserl's view, the crucial issue is naturalism and the problems it poses when it becomes the predominant way of interpreting the world.

It is naturalism, simply put, that is indigenous to the technological worldview and renders it socially problematic. Husserl links the naturalistic prejudice to what he calls the "technization" of knowledge. He writes that knowledge for technicians is "nothing but an artful invention of thinking for purposes of artful achievements in the practice of controlling nature and man." In contrast to this, Husserl avers that genuine knowledge consists of insight and understanding, not manipulation and control. This means that the fundamental concern of a philosophy of technology must be how to render technology intelligible, rather than to control it. .

The impact of Husserl's phenomenology of the life-world will become visible and will be assessed as a basis for establishing a philosophy of technology. In this sense, phenomenology offers the necessary perspective for the philosophy of technology to be based on the human imperative and not vice versa. The final section will discuss what can and cannot be expected from phenomenology as an approach to conceptualizing technology, for this philosophy is not a panacea for all the deleterious effects associated with technological development. Phenomenology does provide, however, an "attitude" that brings technology into focus as problematic and thus supplies a first step toward dealing thoughtfully with this phenomenon.

THE TECHNOLOGICAL WORLD-VIEW

The technological world-view has become pervasive and so permanently fixed that it threatens to occlude other possible ways of relating to the environment. In other words, the myth of technology is so deeply ingrained that persons have forgotten that it offers but one way of viewing the world. Herein lies both the enormous power and danger of technology.

Jacques Ellul has done much to bring technology into focus as a serious matter for philosophical reflection and continues to influence much of the current thinking on this topic. Ellul speaks of the all-encompassing aspect of the technological system outside of which no one can presumably stand. Consequently, Ellul states somewhat paradoxically: "Man is still perfectly capable of choosing, deciding, altering, direction . . . but always within the technological framework and toward the progression of technology." This passage is tantamount to saying that the human capacity to choose or decide-in short, personal freedom-is an illusion.

If this is correct, then everything, goals, options, philosophies, is determined in advanced by the technological system. Precisely how far Ellul would like to take this line of reasoning is unclear, but there is an undeniable cloud of pessimism surrounding his analysis. For now, it is sufficient to note that Ellul's formulation of the central problem confronting the philosophy of technology makes such an undertaking impossible.

Edward Ballard articulates this problem in the following manner: "We who undertake the measure of technological culture have ourselves been formed by that culture." Although he does not succumb to the pessimism found in Ellul, Ballard does not offer a radical method for achieving a perspective above the technological framework. Ballard does employ a "partial epoche" to cope with some of the obstacles to reflecting on technology, but he eschews the phenomenological reduction, or radical reflection, that is necessary for this task.

Ballard, Ellul, and Skolimowski indicate that the urgency of a philosophical investigation of technology stems not from the ill effects of any particular technology but from the technological world-view that displaces all others. This philosophical problem cannot be resolved by adding new and better technologies, for strictly speaking what is problematic is not a technological issue. Moreover, if it is true that persons remain hopelessly tied to the technological framework, then in principle a critical stance can never be taken toward technology.

It might be helpful to look at the matter from a different perspective. If the technological world-view has a prejudicial character, then it follows all self understanding will be affected by it. Indeed, what is really at stake is genuine self-understanding, whereby individuals become aware of themselves as "persons," instead of having a technologically inscribed identity. The contention is not that technology and person are antithetical but that the technological worldview displaces personalistic values. There are a number of ways in which this displacement is manifested.

One symptom is the reversal of the means-end relation, whereby an intrinsic end is reinterpreted gradually as a means. According to Jose Ortega y Gasset, technology is born out of the human need not merely to live but to live well. From its origin, technology is dedicated to well-being, yet a transformation takes place whereby technology is no longer a means to enrich a person's life. Instead, human life is placed in service of technology. The current orientation of higher education in the United States is an example of the consequences of this transformation. Despite rhetoric to the contrary, "education" is regarded by many as a means to prepare individuals for a role in the technological system.

The few who still conceive of education as a means to personal development and the humanization of society recognize that the recent interest in "excellence in education" is rooted primarily in the fear that America's edge in technology may be eroding. Another example of the confusion over the correct arrangement between the demands of technology and "personhood" is the prevalent misunderstanding of leisure as nothing more than recreation. In Aristotle *Politics*, "leisure" provides for personal and moral development, while "recreation" offers a period of repose from occupation. According to this view, recreation, not leisure, is clearly for the sake of work and occupation. In terms of the technological worldview, however, leisure is just another word for idle play, because only work that can be measured is assumed to be significant.

One final way in which the personalistic attitude is displaced by technology can be noted. The technological world-view is characterized by a marked tendency toward calculation and quantification, as though these constitute the only suitable methods for dealing with the physical and socio-cultural environment. In line with this type of thinking, Hermann Meyer asserts: "The way of technology is thus everywhere characterized by the triumph of the calculable over the unpredictable, the abstract over the intuitive-concrete, the functional over the . . . intrinsic value of things . . . and the controllable flow of events [*Ablaufs*] over the free activity of things."

This account is noteworthy because it illustrates the price extracted for the triumph of the technological way of thinking. Although few today would disagree that there is much about human beings that can be quantified and predicted, nevertheless, the expression "person" denotes something of intrinsic value, unique, and not amenable to technological thinking. To summarize the remarks made thus far: Skolimowski is correct that some sort of detachment from the technological world-view is necessary in order to properly understand, assess, and direct technology.

However, the procedures he offers for confronting the technological with nontechnological world-views are inadequate for securing the requisite "detached" perspective. A more fruitful approach is needed; one that reveals the attitude that sustains the technological world-view and exposes that outlook as impoverishing pluralism. Although the path is not Skolimowski's, technology must be made "subject to the human imperative rather than man subject to the technological imperative." What is it; however, that provides the foundation for the reductionistic world-view of technology?

NATURALISM, TECHNOLOGY, AND THE LIFE-WORLD

Commonly, it is asserted that an intimate bond exists between the present technological world-view and the natural scientific conception of nature proposed in the 17th century by Galileo and Descartes. According to Galileo, the universe is a "grand book . . . written in the language of mathematics, and its characters are triangles, circles, and other geometric figures." This "book of nature" metaphor is, of course, consistent with the quantification that characterizes the technological attitude. In order to be fruitful, however, this mathematical scheme requires an accompanying methodological procedure that abstracts the primary qualities from objects. Such a process enables those qualities to be quantified.

Descartes also characterizes matter as an extended substance, with properties such as figure, magnitude, and motion. Likewise, he holds that all natural phenomena are explainable in terms of geometry and mathematics. The outstanding aspect of Descartes' position is his conviction that the knowledge of the "force and . . . action of fire, water, air, the stars, heaven, and all other bodies that environ us" will render persons the "master and possessors of nature." Although it is uncertain whether Descartes means that knowledge encourages manipulation of the environment, his position engenders an attitude toward nature that is compatible with the technological world-view.

In order to avoid misunderstanding, it must be pointed out that the natural scientific and technological attitudes are correlative. Natural science is not necessarily the precondition for a technological world-view. Other crucial factors are necessary before the technological attitude can become the predominant way of thinking. Furthermore, as Martin Heidegger argues, it may be that the technological way of thinking is ontologically, if not chronologically, prior to science. It is sufficient to suggest that the modern technological attitude thrives on the principles of natural science because they share an impoverished view of nature.

From this position of agreement, Husserl's call for a phenomenological analysis of the life-world can be appreciated as a fruitful way to deal with one of the central problems posed by the technological world-view. In this context, the term life-world refers to the realm of experience that constitutes a person's everyday life. When Husserl refers to experience as the base of knowledge, he does not mean that consciousness is just a conduit for information. Instead, he is undercutting the dualism of Descartes and suggesting that consciousness shapes knowledge. What this indicates is that all phenomena are mediated fully by consciousness, while none can claim a seignorial status.

Any form of knowledge that is given primacy over others achieves this position due to a shift in valuation. All knowledge, therefore, receives its meaning through the constitutive activity of human experience. The resulting world is living (life-world), as opposed to one that consists of objective things and events. Because technology is also a product of human experience, or the life-world, it is placed in the service of humanity and cannot define existence. In other words, the technological worldview is illustrated to be one among many ways of interpreting the world. This means that the power of technology to manipulate reality is significantly reduced.

Most important at this juncture is not technology per se but the prejudicial world-view that sustains it and eventually chokes off other ways of relating to the world. When nature is substituted for reality, and the mathematical model of natural science is regarded as the exclusive avenue to truth, genuine science is abandoned in favour of the prejudice of naturalism. The technological and naturalistic attitudes share the tendency to exclude others' ways of viewing the surrounding world. More importantly, they tend to occlude the fact that they are basically intellectual achievements. In so doing, they overlook the fact that the technological-scientific world-view does not constitute an ultimate reality. But, as Langdon Winner observes, technology "contains an inherent tendency toward forgetfulness."

Husserl's meditations on Galilean physics in the *Crisis* confirm Winner's contention that technology is a *"license toforget."* According to Husserl, the Galilean project technologizes science, as one need only to apply the rules of the method to obtain results and not know or remember their purpose. The Galilean enterprise is characterized by yet another sort of forgetfulness: "In geometrical and natural scientific mathematization . . . we measure the lifeworld-the world constantly given to us as actual in our concrete world-life-for a well-fitting *grab of ideas,* that of the so-called objectively scientific truths."

According to Husserl, "we take for *true* being what actually a method is," while the "grab of ideas" displaces the life-world of immediate experience and obtains the ontological status of a true reality. Again, it is not natural science, or even the mathematization of nature that poses a problem, for the success of technology in improving social existence is clear. Obviously, there is a dimension of the life-world that lends itself to mathematization. But this is not the same as saying that reality itself is a mathematical nexus of events or that the world can be expressed only through mathematical or quantitative techniques. It is only against this misinterpretation that Husserl's critique is directed.

Undoubtedly, there are those who would protest that scientific constructions do not displace the life-world. According to this argument, the life-world is a socio-cultural world, which means that it is capable of absorbing natural science and its products without being eclipsed. This view of the life-world reveals the most crucial aspect of Husserl's reflections on Galilean physics: If the natural scientific attitude becomes the dominant perspective from which the world is viewed, then the life-world of experience must be treated as a mere appearance of the "real" world. The fact that natural science is only a special way of interpreting the world and that its correlate nature is only a cultural formation is not recognized. Hence, social-cultural life is misrepresented as a domain with mathematical dimensions.

Several clues can now be gleaned from Husserl's philosophical insights, which help to address the problem of how to achieve a perspective above the technological *Weltanschauung*. The first pertains to Husserl's critique of the Galilean program. This critique undercuts the primacy usually accorded to nature and the mathematical procedures designed to deal with nature. In so doing, the primacy of the life-world is restored as the ground from which all conceivable scientific and technological activity originates. That is, technology is shown to be merely one modality of human experience. Furthermore, the impropriety of reducing persons to objects that have the status of resources is illustrated.

THE PHENOMENOLOGICAL EPOCHE

Philosophically speaking, Skolimowski is correct in his assessment of what must be done before a philosophy of technology can be formulated: how to get enough distance from one's prejudices (in this case, naturalism and technism) so that they are recognized as prejudices. Husserl offers methods for resolving this dilemma that is the main legacy of Husserlian phenomenology. His method provides access to the world precisely as a life-world, or the concrete world of experience that is always presupposed by both scientific and practical activity.

One way to remove the blinders set up by the technological *Weltanschauung* is to experience nontechnological cultures, where alternative world-views are still vital. To some extent, there is even a temptation to view Husserl's discovery and elaboration of the life-world in this light, even though this line of thought is fraught with problems. For example, the phenomenologist and Husserl commentator Maurice Merleau-Ponty liked to emphasize the enormous influence that the anthropologist Lucien Levy-Bruhl had on the phenomenology of the life-world.

Levy-Bruhl's work on primitive cultures purportedly led Husserl to conclude that the power of imagination, so crucial for the phenomenological method of free variation, would be enhanced greatly by contact with primitive societies and their surrounding worlds. Furthermore, according to Merleau-Ponty, Husserl recognized that access to other societies and their worldviews has to come from reliving (*Nachverstehen*) their experience of the world, rathern than from the imaginative variation of one's own socio-cultural world. Indeed, the latter seems almost to require the former.

Although much of what Merleau-Ponty suggests is correct, a more cautious approach is needed. In the first place, Merleau-Ponty's account of Levy-Bruhl's influence on Husserl may be exaggerated. Historically, Husserl recognized at least as early as *Ideas I*, before he studied Levy-Bruhl's work, that "extraordinary profit can be drawn from the offerings of history, in even more abundant measure from those of art, and especially from poetry . . ." Although Husserl does not mention anthropological insights, nothing precludes its addition to the list of things that enrich persons' imaginative powers.

A second, more important problem with Merleau-Ponty's interpretation of Husserl's position, relates to the implication that persons can gain access to an alien world while their own view remains intact. Evidence that this is not a correct interpretation of Husserl can be found in his writings on the mythical convictions of others: "If I retain my faith . . . then their faith is superstition, and if I retain my existing world, then theirs does not exist." Clearly, Husserl is aware that one must suspend belief in his or her own societal world-view before another can be comprehended. Thus, philosophical reflection on and an assessment of the prevailing technological world-view cannot be founded simply upon anthropological or crosscultural studies.

Instead of a comparative study of world-views, the Crisis submits that an epoche or bracketing, of the scientific technological world-view is necessary. The epoche excludes judgments on the truth of scientific theories and knowledge, the value of their aim, and the validity of the form of knowledge that sustains them. In other words, the epoche is a type of radical reflection that allows persons to examine phenomena in terms of how they are experienced, as opposed to how they are supposed to appear according to theories, experts, or other authorities. Furthermore, this style of reflection demonstrates that knowledge cannot be extricated from experience, thus suggesting that even so-called objective data obtain their meaning from human valuation.

The epoche also shows that acts of human valuation subtend every style of knowledge. This understanding reveals the limited validity of any particular form of world interpretation, thereby portraying existence in a multivalent manner. Yet what is remarkable is that nothing is lost after the performance of the epoche. On the contrary, the objective-scientific world-view becomes available for the first time as a matter for reflection, rather than a set of tenaciously held opinions and prejudices that go unscrutinized. Of course, Ballard has already recognized the potential value of applying a similar epoche to the question of technology.

However, the point is that technology can no longer be treated as a single, more or less isolated issue among the myriad problems facing human existence. The life-world of Western humanity is for all purposes a technological world. As such, it requires a more radical epoche than Ballard offers to achieve the desired philosophical perspective on technology. This new epoche would have to coincide with the complete transcendental epoche invoked by Husserl.

The radical nature of the transcendental epoche lies not only in its suspension of a particular vocational attitude-that of the technician or scientist for exampie-but in that it suspends the naive attitude of everyday life and the concomitant world associated with this attitude. According to Husserl:

What must be shown . . . is that through the epoche a new way of experiencing, of thinking, of theorizing, is opened to the philosopher; here, situated above his own natural being and above natural world, he loses nothing of their being and their objective truths and likewise nothing at all of the spiritual acquisitions of his world-life or those of the world historical communal life; he simply forbids himself-as a philosopher-to continue the whole natural performance of his world-life. . . .

This passage suggests that the transcendental epoche should not be narrowly aligned with any particular philosophical problem or set of problems but viewed as coinciding with philosophical reflection. Still, not everyone accepts the idea that the entire philosophical enterprise rests on the method of epoce, and the spatial metaphor Husserl employs to characterize the position from which all genuine philosophical work must proceed only exacerbates the problem. For some, the universal epoche and the correlative attitude of a "disinterested spectator" standing above the life-world signal a flight from reality and even a "renunciation of the obligations one has toward society as well as himself."

For others, Husserl's discussion of a "disinterested spectator" distorts the fact that philosophers, too, are situated in a socio-cultural world, and a perspective above the life-world remains an empty dream. A defense against the first criticism is not difficult since it rests on a facile misconstrual of the transcendental reduction and its accomplishments. Husserl anticipates this when he writes that through the phenomenological epoche "... it seems that I shall never return to the world and to all those problems of life which led me into philosophy in quest of science as rational and radical reflection on the world and human existence."

Further elaboration discloses that the kind of self-reflection engendered by the epoche does not require that I "turn my back on the world to retreat into an unworldly and, therefore, uninteresting special field of theoretical study." Hence, "detachment" from the life-world pertains to the struggle to bring the life-world and its problems into focus as philosophical problems, rather than socio-political, technological, or engineering issues. Moreover, since many modern problems result from the technological *Weltanschauung*, it would seem that some radical new approach such as phenomenological reflection is urgently needed.

Other scholars have recognized already the importance of the phenomenological method and, in some instances; have employed it in their philosophical examinations of technology. The present problem, however, is more fundamental for it concerns the possibility of a genuine philosophy of technology. The primary intention has been to recapture the philosophical ethos embodied in the Husserlian conception of phenomenology and the method of epoche. This raises the second criticism of the phenomenological reduction, which argues that the reduction is destined to remain an empty dream because philosophers are also human beings and cannot be uprooted from their socio-historical world. As suggested, this criticism is not warranted in light of Husserl's writing on the subject.

Nonetheless, what bearing, if any, does phenomenological philosophy and reduction have on the theme of this conference; that is, on the relationship between technology and human productivity? If human productivity means nothing more than the production of goods and the efficient utilization of human and natural resources, then phenomenology is at best only remotely relevant. On the other hand, if Ortega y Gasset's opinion is accepted that the fundamental product of technology is man, then the aim and method of phenomenology play a crucial role in understanding the relationship between technology and human productivity.

Phenomenology is crucial because one of its principal aims is to restore the personalistic attitude and, therefore, persons and the lived-world to a place of preeminence vis-à-vis the natural scientific and technological attitudes. It is also crucial because the radical self-reflection that comes with the performance of the phenomenological epoche is central to the notion of person as autonomous and self-responsible. Nonetheless, what about the possibility of the phenomenological epoche or reduction? Suppose that Husserl's critics are correct and an actual execution of a reduction is destined to remain a dream, something hoped for but never really attained. Would such a concession render this undertaking meaningless or could the phenomenological epoche still be defended?

Throughout this chapter concern has been expressed with the pervasive technological world-view of present-day culture and with the problem it creates for a philosophy of technology. The real obstacle is how to get above a naive conception of the world as to see it as a philosophical problem. Herein lies the extraordinary value of the phenomenological epoche. Generally speaking, the method of reduction does not lead directly to solutions for social and life-world problems. However, in its role of suspending the natural attitude it illustrates such problems and, at the same time, brings all mundane solutions and analyses of life-world problems into focus as problematic. Maurice Natanson recognizes this aspect of the Husserlian program when he writes: "It is not his [Husserl's] claim that sounding the alarm is equivalent to putting out the fire, but he has demonstrated what is wrong with a culture which no longer recognizes alarms. . ."

From this point of view, phenomenology's most significant contribution to the philosophy of technology follows from its transformation of a naive technological mode of interpreting the world into a permanent philosophical problem requiring persistent vigilance. Even if a complete reduction is not possible, the resolve and struggle to suspend the naive attitude of everyday life can nonetheless protect persons from committing two errors frequently connected with technology. The first is the antipathy of some people toward everything technological; the second is the love affair of the majority with everything technological.

Although this may seem like a small gain for so much effort, it must be remembered that the durable and still influential philosophy of Plato rests on the conviction that philosophy and the power of recollection begin with the recognition of ignorance. This is a lesson from phenomenology: Humanity must not be complacent but much search for greater insights by constantly questioning its understanding of technology and the technological *Weltanschauung*.

2

Education

Challenges, Chances, Changes

Being part of an evaluation of the distance teaching system, my research has addressed the teaching system as well as the situation and the learning environment of men and women studying at a distance. The aim of the research was to identify factors which facilitate successful studying and factors which make it more difficult for the students to pursue their educational goals. The identification of these positive and negative aspects is the prerequisite for pointing out the need and direction of institutional changes in order to improve the open and distance learning provision.

As far as women distance students were concerned, the research brought to light some patterns in their personal circumstances and their learning styles as well as in their use of the institutional provision of support services which differed systematically from those of the male distance students. The under-representation of women in tertiary DE in Germany could at least in part be directly attributed to the fact that the FeU did not recognise these gender patterns and therefore failed to accommodate the needs of women distance students to the extent necessary to guarantee equal access and study conditions for both men and women.

In the face of these findings which, moreover, are replicated year after year in new evaluation studies it may seem strange that I talk about the chances which distance education offers to women. Am I whistling in the dark trying to convince myself that all is well? Do I just want to believe that my work has meaning and that distance education can indeed serve the needs of women? Or can we really challenge the existing distance teaching system to become less androcentric and more women-friendly?

CHALLENGES

Distance education is about challenges. On the institutional level, concern with women students and gender issues challenges a distance teaching university to review the study materials, the course contents and presentation, the teaching system, and even the composition of its staff and course authors. Once it is discovered that the seeming neutrality is in fact biased and unfavourable circumstances are created for women, the university is faced with the challenge of developing measures which will ensure equal opportunities in all areas.

It will need to overcome resistance to these changes based partly on a natural inertia favouring the *status quo* and partly on deep-seated attitudes concerning the status of men and women. Some may even question the legitimacy of gender as a category in ODL. The starting point for looking at gender issues at the FeU was the observation that women were extremely under-represented as compared to other German universities, and to DTUs in countries such as Britain and Canada. The reasons for this low rate of participation were usually sought in limited course choices coupled with the continued existence of traditional gendered subject preferences. Both of these factors were assumed to be outside the influence of the university and therefore demanded no action.

From the beginning, our research showed that this was not a sufficient explanation and that other factors were at work hindering women's access to university level DE. In parallel surveys at the OU UK and the FeU empirical evidence was collected which demonstrated a relation between certain characteristics of the distance teaching systems on the one hand and the personal circumstances and learning styles of male and female distance students on the other hand. The data suggested specific areas in which institutional action could reduce the male bias and contribute to a more equitable representation of women. At the FeU, for instance, all of the areas mentioned above did not take gender into account.

This included not only the teaching system and organisation of local support, but also the contents and presentation of courses and the overwhelmingly male academic staff. The question is how to overcome the male bias and implement women-friendly perspectives without, as is often feared, compromising high standards of quality and academic standing.

Whether the challenge of creating an equitable distance education system is taken up and how vigorously it is pursued depends in part on whether the decision-makers see this as a problem which needs to be addressed, or whether they perceive it as an irrelevant side issue, or even an irritant brought up by a few incorrigible feminists. In part, too, outside pressures could build up and create a more urgent need for the university to be seen as an equal opportunities institution. This is the case when part of the government funding is paid out only on the condition of an increased proportion of women enrolling and completing degrees or being promoted to higher staff levels and tenured posts.

At the personal level, becoming a distance student presents more than one challenge. For instance, there is the question of how to fit the distance course into an already busy day, coping with a household and children, possibly a job and other responsibilities. What priorities with regard to family, work and distance studying must be set and what limitations are necessary and acceptable? How can the wish to pursue a course of studies be justified when it threatens to detract from the woman's duties as mother and from her domestic and partnership role? Our research has shown time and again the multiple pressures on women due to their domestic and mothering responsibilities, which often have to be fulfilled in addition to outside paid work and other commitments.

There are many studies which show that the social division of labour has basically remained unchanged along traditional gender lines according to which the full responsibility for the private sphere is assigned to women, with the men occasionally helping with some of the domestic chores and childcare. Even though in countries such as Germany, a socially acceptable attitude of partnership has evolved in the past few decades, in practice this leads to an increase in women's workforce participation, but not to a corresponding increase in men's participation in domestic labour. Distance students, as part of the larger society, *a priori* are no exception.

To mention only some of the consequences, this means that women enrolling in a degree course have to fit it in not only with paid work, but also with family work, thus carrying a double or triple load. An additional challenge results from the fact that the domestic work, especially childcare, is extremely fragmented and difficult to plan, thus making it hard to schedule contiguous blocks of study time and to find the time and space for uninterrupted and concentrated work. On top of that, as research also has shown, the demands made by their families on women distance students increase rather than decrease as is the case with men who enrol in a degree course. It follows that women face a formidable challenge in having to set priorities and negotiate with family and friends their right to 'do their own thing'.

CHANCES

Distance education is about chances. Opportunities of obtaining an education and formal qualifications which were denied earlier in life. Opportunities to pursue a degree without giving up one's job and one's livelihood or disrupting one's career or one's family. Chances of studying while being in a situation which prevents attendance at 'regular' universities, be it a tour in the army, a stay in hospital, a job abroad or without regular hours, a family to take care of, or any other of numerous circumstances which preclude participation in classroom education.

On the face of it, these opportunities are no different for women than they are for men. In some countries, where girls and women are largely excluded from education at all levels, DE may be the only option, as has been reported by colleagues in India, for instance. In reality, as we have seen, the opportunities are not equal since women have to overcome greater odds in order to access a degree programme and face more obstacles in reconciling their distance studies with the other areas of their lives. They have fewer resources but more responsibilities, less support from their family and more scruples about the legitimacy of getting an education for themselves.

In the face of this, are we even justified in assuming that the DE mode offers special opportunities for women in any situation and, especially, for the housebound mothers of small children which the early literature was so fond of? I believe we are. For one thing, women do take the opportunities offered by DE. In spite of all the difficulties and obstacles confronting women in DE, there are many successful students who either complete a degree or gain personal development through studying. Many of these women would not have been able to do this if they could not have done it at a distance.

The expression 'taking a chance' indicates that a certain element of risk is involved in an undertaking. It is part of the DE philosophy that students can enrol in a degree programme without incurring the existential risk entailed in giving up one's job and income in order to attend university. This is true for women who study without risking their jobs, thus maintaining what may be their only source of income or a necessary supplement to the family income. At another level, women are taking a chance when they risk upsetting the balance of power in their own homes. Since it is not possible to study without at least partially changing the routines and taking time out, the family will feel somewhat neglected - and will let the student know what her priorities ought to be.

This, in turn, reinforces her own feelings of guilt which often lead her to try and be an even better housewife and mother than before enrolment. In set-ups like this, with their totally unrealistic expectations, there is a real danger of the woman giving up her education before she has achieved her goals, be they the completion of a formal degree or her personal development. Another problem concerns the question of whether the woman, who often has no recent experience with formal education, feels she is capable of studying successfully or that she will be able to 'learn how to learn'.

How will she cope if she decides to pursue a university degree and does not complete the course or does badly in her exams? Where does she find motivation and energy needed to continue? Again, our research shows gender-specific patterns, since women are more likely to feel that 'failure' in their distance studies obliges them to discontinue and return to devoting their full time and attention to their families. The answers to these questions seem to lie in the support and connection with other students in similar circumstances. This is where the gender differences in learning styles, brought to light through research by and with women, play an important role.

For one thing, finding a group of women to study with can be a tremendous help in the learning process, fulfilling the need for social contact and connectedness. Also, due to the women's movement it has long been known that the sharing and exchanging of individual experiences often leads to the discovery of common patterns and structural discrimination where the isolated woman has felt personally responsible for not being able to cope or for her 'failure' as a mother, a wife, and as it were a distance student. In taking the opportunity to seek out other women and sharing her experience of the difficulties, the lack of study progress, and the fights with her partner, the 'bad' mothering, and the neglected household, with other women, a distance student can find out that this is not her individual shortcoming but an almost automatic and universal pattern. She can also find out how other women deal with this situation.

Together, the women can help each other to develop coping strategies as well as provide more tangible support, such as taking turns babysitting, forming car-pools, joining up on the computer, explaining some of the course-material. Another aspect of the opportunities arising in DE concerns the institution. Our research has not only brought us insights into the way in which women deal with the problems, but also provided information on the measures the institutions of open and distance learning can take in order to facilitate access and success.

This may be of benefit not only to the women but also to the men studying at a distance. For instance, the research on communication preferences and patterns showed an unexpectedly high interest in personal interaction and communication amongst all students. Until then it had often been taken for granted that the typical distance student was not only content to study in the privacy and isolation of the single, unconnected learner, but was actually happy doing this. There are other instances of how a supposedly more women-friendly approach could benefit all students, and in this lies a chance for DTUs to improve their systems for both men and women which surely must be a goal of distance education everywhere.

CHANGES

Distance education is about change. By virtue of their very existence, DTUs change the previously clear structure of the educational system in a given society. If schooling and vocational or professional qualifications are no longer confined to the traditional places of learning, schools and universities lose their monopoly, and restrictions in access to education can no longer be as rigidly enforced. In addition, as access to educational opportunities becomes more fluid, there must also be changes in the social structure, at least in those areas where status and position are conferred on the basis of formal qualifications.

My own research on women from working-class backgrounds confirms that changes of this kind are taking place. In the 1960s race and ethnicity were not yet relevant sociological categories for the analysis of inequality in West German society and in the West German educational system.

Rather, 'Roman Catholic working-class girls living in rural areas' had been identified as the educationally most disadvantaged social group, with extremely low chances of getting secondary schooling and entering university. In the FeU survey which I used for my analysis, many of the working-class women students had obtained their university entrance qualifications - a prerequisite for enrolling in a degree course - via evening classes and 'second-chance' schools.

They were employed in dead-end, boring jobs which provided a basic income and a certain degree of highly valued security, but did not offer career prospects or intellectual challenges. In choosing to study for a degree at a distance these women could pursue a dream of upward occupational and social mobility and of personal development which would not have been possible in any other university setting.

Conducting an earlier small-scale interview study of three randomly chosen women graduates, Irene Raehlmann found that all three women happened to be of working-class origin. Her analysis of the in-depth interviews led her to conclude that all had been highly motivated to break out of their 'inherited' class position and on the basis of their studying and gaining their M.A. had brought about changes in their personal and professional lives. DE has other important functions for women which obviously makes it worth their while.

They use their newly acquired formal qualification to enter or re-enter the labour market after a period of raising children, they break out of a dead-end job, or they get started on a new career or promoted to a higher position. Sometimes, of course, their expectations are not met and the hoped-for changes do not materialise in the labour-market for which they may be considered too old by the time they finish their studies or not experienced enough in the field they want to enter.

One of the most profound changes which can happen through DE is connected to the challenges mentioned above with respect to the domestic and family situation. There is, rightly, some concern over the possibility that DE could reinforce the traditional role of women being responsible for household and childcare and relegated to the private sphere. Home study, which can be pursued without entering the public sphere, could serve to 'keep women in their place' and to 'domesticate' them even further in accordance with traditional cultural values and social norms.

While we have to keep this possibility in mind and make sure countermeasures are taken to prevent it happening, it is likely that the liberating potential will be the stronger of the two forces inherent in ODL. For one thing, it has been noted that education as such serves to empower women. This may be on the most basic level through literacy programmes, or on more advanced levels through university study and even Ph.D. programmes. As recently as March 1998, for instance, a UNICEF study on violence against women in south-east Asia concluded that compulsory schooling for all girls would be a long-term measure to reduce violence against women by providing them with qualifications as the basis for getting a job which in turn would enable them to earn their own income and improve their status.

Simultaneously, they propagate a campaign to educate the general populace about human rights and the need for attitude changes toward women. Returning to the family situation of women distance students, we find that many more or less far-reaching changes take place. Not all of these were probably intended from the start, and some may not be welcome. Taking up a course of studies invariably affects the private arrangements and domestic division of labour and the way in which the woman sees her role and sets her priorities. In order to study successfully, the woman has to try and organise her time differently; she must find a space in which she can study without being disturbed; and she must spread at least some of her household chores and childcare responsibilities around.

This means getting her partner, older children, parents and friends to take over chores such as doing the dishes, the laundry and the shopping, or dropping the kids off at nursery school, to mention just a few. Even in cases where the student tries to change as little of her routine as possible, there will be times when she has to prepare for exams or attend a seminar, or when she is simply too tired and exhausted or too frustrated to be as patient as she might wish to be or as her family expects her to be. There is some evidence that it might be better to become aware of these kinds of things early on and negotiate demands and support with one's family, including the use of family resources such as the car for visits to the study centre and the PC for communication and course work.

Another change which has been observed relates to aspects of personal development. Many women enter DE unsure of their ability to study at university level or uncertain whether they could master their chosen subject. Their success in doing it increases their self-esteem and their study progress provides them with a broader knowledge and more self-confidence. Family women who do not also have a job outside the home can profit from joining self-help study groups as has been shown in a project providing a support infrastructure for mothers of young children.

The participants, who started out as isolated housewives with little self-esteem and not much control over their domestic situation, eventually became self-confident emancipated women who claimed their own study space and time and their right to pursue their chosen course. Finally, there are those changes which occur on the institutional level. Some of those are apparent, such as the shift in emphasis from distance teaching to open and distance learning and the increase in flexibility and learner-centredness this implies.

In the 1990s there has been an increasing concern with quality assurance in distance education which is part of this shift, but also must be seen in the context of fiscal and administrative control over the use of resources. Some changes are very rapid and seemingly inevitable, such as the increased use of ICTs, which transform not only the organisation of the DE systems but also have an impact on the design of teaching materials and media and on the target groups.

The use of the internet and the electronic highway is envisioned to lead to the establishment of the electronic campus and the virtual university which, via the world-wide web, has global connections. Other changes are more gradual and less automatic. They depend on attitude shifts and new policy decisions. Among these is the change from androcentric to women-friendly distance education, i.e. from gender-blind DE systems and pedagogy to an awareness of gender as an important category. Let us continue to whistle in the dark! Not in order to pretend all is well, but because others will hear us and take notice.

LEARNING STYLES AND LOCAL SUPPORT SERVICES

Both the distance teaching system and the different circumstances of women's and men's lives affect their chances to enrol in and complete a DE course of studies. This chapter deals with the learning styles of women and men and with the different ways in which they use the support services provided by the institution as part of the distance teaching environment. Drawing on research data from Britain and Germany, this chapter is concerned with gender differences in students' approach to their distance studies and in the use of study centres and local support services.

It is largely based on the joint analysis of data from parallel research done by Gill Kirkup at the OU UK and by Ute Rossie and myself at the FeU in the 1980s which offered the first empirical evidence of the relevance of gender in open and distance learning provision. Although the data on which this analysis was based is some twelve years old, it is by no means outdated. Surveys done in the intervening years have repeatedly confirmed the continued existence of gender differences in study behaviour and the importance of taking these divergent learning styles into account.

A recent example is a study on interaction in DE which Mary Davoust (1996) carried out in Sweden and which showed 'a significant difference between men and women in the answers about the interaction. Women state a higher need in general.' At the FeU the most recent evaluation of learning styles and support services was a 1996 survey on student use and appreciation of study centres and tutorial services. The results once again demonstrated the validity of our earlier conclusions that support and connectedness characterise the learning styles of women distance students in a way which differs from the learning styles of the male distance students.

THEORETICAL AND EMPIRICAL CONTEXT

By its very character, the distance mode is open to scrutiny to a much greater extent than other types of university, where the teaching takes place behind the closed doors of lecture halls and seminar rooms, and where examinations are usually conducted within the walls of the ivory tower. As a new and different mode of learning and teaching, DE has always been open to experimentation and to didactical and pedagogical development. This is both because of the (mostly) indirect teaching methods required, and also the fact that distance students at tertiary level are mature adults. The recent flood of changes in education has happened in the wake of the technological revolution, which has already had profound effects on the dissemination of knowledge and on communication across time and space.

Much has been written about the didactics and pedagogy of DE, a recent publication being an overview by Otto Peters (1998) entitled *Learning and Teaching in Distance Education. Pedagogical Analyses andInterpretations in an International Perspective.* As a sociologist and an institutional researcher I am not an expert on teaching methods, pedagogy, or learning psychology. My concern is with the practice of DE following the application of these disciplines, and with their consequences for the adults studying at a distance. In this context the question arises of whether we can identify factors which make learning at a distance either easier or more difficult for women and whether the pedagogy of teaching at a distance needs to become gender-sensitive to an extent that renders it women-friendly.

The focus on women as learners in a DE setting was a prerequisite for discovering the existence of both gendered learning styles and the consequent need for DE institutions to take the learning styles of adult women into account. It provided the framework for our analysis of the empirical data on women and men studying at a distance in Germany and Britain and has contributed to the increasing concern among distance educators, mainly women, with 'the importance of gender as a category in open and distance learning' and, more specifically, with 'women as learners' and with the consequent 'issues for visual and virtual classrooms'.

In comparing data from the OU UK and the German FeU, Gill Kirkup and I were aware of the fact that the two DTUs are quite different in their teaching systems, although both are single-mode institutions with very large student populations. In spite of the different distance education systems and social contexts in the two countries, our preliminary data analysis showed similar patterns in the responses of FeU and OU UK students. There were parallels on two levels:

1. The comparison of men and women in each study yielded similar gender differences; and
2. The comparison of the responses of the two groups of women distance students yielded similar answering patterns. The similarities occurred with respect to the study behaviour, the use of study centres and the relevance which students assigned to local support services provided through tutors (mentors), counsellors, study groups, and other students.

Women distance students in both countries valued support and connectedness much more than their male colleagues did. This means that women are more interested in interpersonal contacts with other students and with staff members. They consequently visit study centres more frequently, have higher attendance rates at tutorials and study groups, and are more interested in face-to-face meetings with other students and teaching staff and in all forms of cooperative learning. In short, the comparative data analysis showed that, unlike the male students, women distance students in the FeU as well as the OU UK preferred to do their studying in a connected and social context.

By comparing the data from our two surveys Gill Kirkup and I realised that the gender patterns in the answers of the students in Britain and Germany was not simple coincidence, but reflected systematic differences in the learning styles of men and women. We found convincing arguments in the work of Gilligan, J. Thompson and Belenky, Clinchy, Goldberger and Tarule which proved very useful for the understanding of the empirical phenomena in our joint surveys. Jane Thompson's *Learning Liberation. Women's Response to Men's Education* provides a picture of the learning processes of women in face-to-face situations which are based on the principle of shared learning.

In their preference for this learning style, the women distance students in Germany and Britain resemble the adult women in Jane Thompson's description of adult and continuing education. Carol Gilligan's *In a Different Voice: Psychological Theory and Women's Development*, and Mary F. Belenky and her colleagues' *Women's Ways of Knowing: The Development of Self, Voice, and Mind* supplied the theoretical framework for the analysis of the observed gender differences. In referring to this framework we were not interested in joining the feminist debate on equality and difference or in using our data to prove one or the other position in this debate.

We were interested in understanding the gender differences in the participation in distance education, including the under-representation of women students in Germany as well as the differences in study behaviour and learning styles in both countries.

Our situation as researchers on women in DE was characterised by the fact that before the mid-1980s gender issues had not been a topic for institutional research in open and distance learning contexts. The book *Toward New Horizons for Women in Distance Education*, edited by Karlene Faith in 1988, was the first international collection of contributions about gender relations in DE settings. Until that time, as Elizabeth J. Burge points out in her foreword to the book, a total of six papers with a gender focus had been published in the two major international journals, *Teaching at a Distance* and *Distance Education*.

In her keynote address to the 1995 Cambridge Conference entitled *Putting the Student First. Learner-Centred Approaches in Open and Distance Learning*, Gill Kirkup described the history of gender research in ODL and its connection with our own work. The material collected by Karlene Faith supported our impression that our findings had a broader significance and were not limited to the OU UK and FeU contexts:

> Before the Faith book there had been a commonly accepted view that ODL is a type of education that is particularly suited to women ... The historical material discussed above suggests that this view was reasonably founded in the knowledge that adult women have many more restrictions on their time and mobility than adult men, as well as their access to disposable income, which made ODL the most practical option for post-school education. However, there is often an implicit presumption that, apart from these material factors, women are the same as men with respect to their motivations to study and their intellectual styles, as well as their domestic circumstances.

The assumption that equal opportunities exist for women and men to enter programmes of distance and open learning and that they have equal chances to complete a degree easily leads to a deficit model in the face of the under-representation of women among the students and especially among the graduates of DTUs. In an androcentric frame of reference, study behaviour and learning styles which are different from that of men are usually perceived as inferior or less mature, and consequently women have been seen as being on a lower level of intellectual and moral development. In this model, the action required of the institution to redress the gender imbalances is directed at bringing women up to the standard which is seen as universally valid.

It was the search for alternative explanations which led us to the above-mentioned work of Gilligan, J. Thompson and Belenky *et al.* They provide a frame of reference which does not measure women by a male standard of which, almost inevitably, they must fall short. The discovery that women develop in different ways from men allows us to accept the validity of their experience and to start looking into the previously neglected question of how DE systems can serve the needs of women students. In this model, the action required by the institution to redress gender imbalances is directed at changing the teaching system to suit the learning styles of women as well as those of men:

This connected way of being for women comes, it is argued [by Gilligan], out of a life in which one's relationships with others are a crucial part of personal development. It is a positive way of being rather than an immature state on the road to 'separation' or 'independence' which is how it was previously described. Belenky *et al*.... describe women as 'connected knowers' who, when they reach the highest stages of intellectual development, equivalent to but not the same as those described by Perry, continue to exhibit a strong sense of relatedness to others. Something lacking in men at the same stage.

The comparative findings on the study behaviour of men and women could all be explained using the concepts of support and connectedness: the fact that women visit study centres and use local support services more frequently in spite of having to overcome more obstacles, the higher value they place on social learning and connectedness with other students, the greater feelings of isolation in being a distance student - all of these fit into the picture of women having a 'connected way of being'.

The work of other colleagues on women in ODL has since confirmed the empirical and theoretical value of this model for gender analysis. In a recent article, Elizabeth J. Burge sums up some of the newer findings:

Distance education discussions about women's learning add to the already large body of research into women's learning in 'traditional' walled classrooms, ... into the preferred relational styles of many women learners (compared to the autonomous styles preferred by many men learners), and the ways in which women come to know what they know

We can expect that when helping many women to make a successful comeback into higher education and develop learning to learn skills, we have to focus less on the three 'Rs' of receive, retain, and return, and more on respect, re-frame and re-apply, so that the relevant knowledge is generated and used.

We will therefore continue to use this theoretical framework both in our individual research and in future comparative projects. One of the research issues which will become increasingly important for institutional and evaluation research is the rapidly developing field of information and communication technologies (ICTs). Already, studies have shown gender differences in access, control and use of the new media which in the traditional androcentric manner are explained in terms of the deficit model. We suggest that it is extremely important to apply the gendered learning style model to this field in order to develop the technologies in a way that ensures gender equity in the 'virtual university' of the future. For instance, we need:

To look at different attitudes that men and women students have towards the new (and old) ODL technologies that we are experimenting with - if not fully committed to - in our various institutions ... The model we have used is certainly not post-modernist and is open to criticism that it could be interpreted as essentialist. The question is whether it is supported by empirical data, and whether it can provide any help in deciding future strategies for both women and men using ICTs in ODL.

The following sections of this chapter provide empirical data on the gender differences in students' use of study centres and local support services and the higher value women place on this support. The findings, some of which have already been presented in joint contributions and in FeU research reports, are taken from our parallel surveys and from evaluation studies at the FeU.

GENDER AND STUDY CENTRE ATTENDANCE

In order to evaluate the use distance students make of study centres it is necessary to look at the institutional provision of a local support infrastructure and at the services available to students in different regions of the country. These are based on the institutional policy regarding the role of decentralised services in a distance teaching system. The geographical distribution of study centres in Germany as well as student numbers shows a regional disparity which is due to the fact that each of the states (or provinces) of the Federal Republic is responsible for its own education system.

In order to establish local support services outside NRW, the state government has to negotiate treaties with other Provincial (e.g. Bavaria) or foreign (e.g. Austria) governments. As a result, the situation in NRW roughly parallels that of the OU UK, while other regions such as Bavaria offer only few opportunities for students to access local support. The unequal geographical distribution is reflected in the results of a 1996 survey on study centre use, which showed that 83% of the students in NRW (the home state of the FeU), but only 57% of the students living in other regions reported living within easy reach of a study centre.

Overall, two-thirds of the respondents (66%) lived within easy reach of a study centre; three out of ten (30%) lived not far from a study centre which would have been difficult to reach; and only 4% lived totally outside the catchment area of an FeU study centre (von Prümmer 1997b). This may be due to an increase in the number of study centres maintained by the FeU, but certainly is a reflection of the composition of the groups of respondents which must be considered biased in favour of study centre attendees.

Considering the uneven geographical distribution of study centres in Germany, these answers must be interpreted to mean that the survey, which explicitly concerned the use of local support services, addressed significantly fewer students who had no way of using these services in the first place and therefore do not feel competent to judge their value. In addition, there might be different interpretations of what it means to be 'near to' or 'within reach of' a study centre; and students who objectively live some distance from a centre might consider it 'within easy reach' because they are used to travelling long distances, or because they have fast and comfortable means of transport.

The decision to attend a study centre is influenced by a number of factors rooted both in institutional provision and in the personal circumstances of individual students. It should be noted that the data reported here do not permit statistical conclusions about the situation in East Germany due to the small number of respondents from the former German Democratic Republic - only 66 respondents from the five new states participated in the survey. Apart from the constraints put on distance students through their employment and family responsibilities, study centre attendance is dependent on factors such as availability and access to study centres, and on students' knowledge of local support services and on their view of the possible benefits and costs associated with attending.

The following quotes illustrate the way in which students feels that insufficient information prevents their making full or better use of the local support services offered by the university. All the comments in this chapter, which are a very small sample of the comments given in answer to open questions, are from women students who participated in the 1996 survey on the use and value of study centres and tutorial support at the FeU.

'Students should be informed about all seminars and tutorials relevant for preparing for examinations, regardless of where in Germany they happen to be held. As a student one is quite willing to sacrifice a weekend and travel long distances in order to get the best possible exam preparation!'

'I wish to have more information about seminars and tutorials in other places, not just my own study centre. In this way I could plan my schedule to fit them in. Since I am currently commuting between Dortmund and Düsseldorf every day, I could easily attend different study centres and profit from their services.'

'Since a large number of courses are offered in my subject area by the Department of Education, Social Sciences and Humanities, there are many courses without tutorial support. If I had more detailed information about the tutoring/ counselling offered in neighbouring study centres (and if the

FeU employed more tutors/mentors), this would alleviate the situation somewhat.'

Other students refer to the expected benefits in relation to the expenditure of time and money involved in attending study centres and face-to-face sessions. The following quotes from students who do not frequent a study centre show that they are likely to discontinue their attendance or to attend only specific events if they consider the costs to outweigh the gains for their study progress. There were also those students who no longer attended tutorials in the study centre during the semester but who felt that they would benefit from more concentrated sessions such as weekend seminars:

'I find weekend seminars or week-long summer schools, which are specifically directed at preparing for the examination in a given subject, much more useful than non-specific evening tutorials which cover a whole range of topics. These seminars offer the chance to get away from one's daily domestic stress and to study specific issues intensively. Also, in these cases one gets the most benefit out of the journey, which is usually quite time-consuming. On top of this I find it difficult to find a childminder on week-day evenings.'

'I am very unhappy with the fact that [the state/province of] Hessen does not offer tutorial support to the same extent as does NRW. In order to attend specific seminars for the exam preparation in my subjects I have to travel to Aurich or other towns in northern Germany. This is a very great outlay both financially and timewise.'

'Tutorial support in my study centre is mostly limited to first- and second-year courses. But it is in those study centres which are quite a distance from the centre in Hagen, that support in more advanced courses is essential. I am certain that many students would attend weekend seminars with teaching staff from Hagen and that they would consider them worthwhile even if they had to travel long distances. As it is now, many students, especially those living in Baden-Württemberg and Bavaria [southern Germany], have high costs and time-consuming journeys, even having to take leave days, in order to attend one-day seminars which are scheduled for workdays.'

'There should be more week-end seminars outside of NRW to avoid discrimination of students living in other states/provinces and who have to invest much more money and time and need a lot more motivation to attend. Such seminars are very important since they often are the only human contact with the FeU.'

'If you come from a rural area and have children it is nearly impossible to attend tutorials or seminars on a regular basis as the costs (childcare) and time (long distances) is too great. Absolutely desirable: weekend seminars (Friday-Sunday) in all FeU study centres (including Frankfurt). There are study centres in northern Germany which do wonderful work but are too far, which leads to high costs and the question of childcare.'

The 1986 data on geographical distribution showed no differences in study centre attendance between women and men enrolled at the OU UK or at the FeU in Germany. Yet in both countries we found that significantly more women than men report longer journeys to their study centre with 36% of the men, but only 29% of the women taking less than half an hour to travel. At the same time women were more frequent users of the local services. This was as true in 1996 as it was ten years earlier and can be demonstrated by looking at those distance students who report easy access to a study centre and thus may be assumed to have equal chances of attending.

The most recent figures show that half of the FeU students with easy access to a study centre visit it on a regular basis, with 9% more women (56%) than men (47%) being regular users. Fewer than four out of ten FeU students attend a study centre on a casual basis, and women (36%) and men (39%) are nearly equally likely to report occasional visits. In accordance with the earlier findings, men were more apt to refrain altogether from attending (11%) than women (6.5%) even when a study centre was within easy reach. Other factors related to frequency of attendance are major subject area and students' motivation to obtain a university degree through their distance studies.

Attendance in study centres also depends on the means of transport students' use for travelling. This is most often the car owned by the student or by a family member, and here we found that women are less likely than men to have full control over this important resource. A comparison of 1996 survey data to earlier findings shows more use of public transport. This may be due to better transport provision or changed locations of study centres. It may also reflect social changes such as an increased concern with environmental issues which leads to a shift away from the use of private cars. The quantitative data and the quotes in this and the following sections of this chapter are taken from the 1996 FeU survey on study centres and tutorial support.

As was the case in previous research, students often experience transport problems in conjunction with other factors. Some difficulties faced by women in this respect are expressed in the following quotes:

'It is relatively time-consuming (a total of 2 hours travelling time for 80 km, parking problems).'

'This is due exclusively to the travelling situation as public transport is poor or non-existent. The study centre is only accessible for local people or for people with a car. Therefore I rarely can attend tutorials. Getting a lift is an exceptional happening.'

'I am very satisfied with the services and equipment provided in the study centre, as well as with the staff who are very helpful. The reason why I attend so rarely is in no way the fault of any deficits on the part of the study centre. Rather, it is due to my personal/domestic situation: two children aged 7 and years, a husband working shifts, only one car in the family, and a circle of friends and acquaintances who have little tolerance for my studying.'

'Regrettably there is no tutorial support I can use!!! I can reach a study centre easily (only 20 minutes by car) but it only offers tutorial support and face-to-face seminars in first- and second-year courses. To reach the nearest study centre which provides tutorial support in advanced courses I have to drive for over an hour. But some seminars or tutorials start so early (5:00-6:00 p.m.) that I cannot get there in time after work, due to the long drive. This is the reason why I attend this study centre rarely, although I would like to go more often.'

'During the advanced phase of my degree programme I have used a study centre quite often, but so far this has been limited to exam preparations in one subject. The problem is that the study centre which offers relevant tutoring/counselling can be reached only by car without too great a loss of time. Since I cannot drive myself, attendance is difficult for me. So far, the tutorial support which I have been able to use has been good and helpful for my exam preparations.'

The role of local support services for beginning students varies between the different academic departments of the FeU, and this is reflected in subject-related attendance patterns. Students enrolled in the Economics Department, for instance, find a wide range of course-related and exam-oriented tutorials available at most study centres. Regular attendance is therefore possible in regions with study centres. Students enrolled in degree programmes in the Department of Education, Social Sciences and Humanities on the other hand, are offered a range of individual seminars and tutorials on a one-off basis. It is therefore not surprising to find that 53% of the economics students but only 38% of the humanities students (education, social sciences and humanities) attended the study centre in their vicinity.

Within each of these two degree areas, women with easy access to a study centre were more frequent attendees than men, the difference being 14.9 percentage points in economics, and 10.9 percentage points in the humanities.Because of the small numbers of respondents, especially women, in the other degree programmes we looked at all students living near an FeU study centre, even if they themselves felt that getting there is time-consuming or expensive. In this case, all academic departments showed the same gendered attendance patterns with more women visiting study centres on a regular basis than men. This is true for:

- The Department of Economics (women 51.8%; men 39.5%; difference Ä=12.3%; n = 1.053);
- The Department of Education, Social Sciences and Humanities (women 34.0%; men 24.2%; Ä=9.8%; n= 255);
- The Department of Computer Science (women 41.5%; men 38.6%; Ä=2.9%; n= 168).

Since only ten women enrolled in the Department of Mathematics and nine women enrolled in the Department of Electrical Engineering participated in the survey, no gender analysis is possible for these degree programmes. Again, this data confirms the fact that women distance students tend to overcome larger odds in their willingness to participate in face-to-face learning processes and meet with other students and teaching staff, as the following student quotes illustrate:

'If only there were tutorial supports for law courses! And if only my study centre had a meeting room (lounge, cafeteria) where I could bring my child and work without too much hassle.'

'Since entering the advanced phase of my degree programme I have not been to a study centre, as the three study centres in my area don't offer tutorial support for courses in mathematics and computer science (unfortunately!!). I really wish these services could be improved. PS: A suggestion - all study centres should be equipped with computers which allow access to the library catalogue, just like the terminals in the FeU library in Hagen.' 'The study centre would have played a larger role in my studies if there had been more tutorials/ seminars in my field.'

One of the most important factors influencing a student's decision to spend the time and effort visiting a study centre is their determination to complete a degree (degree orientation). Four out of ten women (40%), and three out of ten men (33%) studying at the FeU say that it is 'absolutely necessary' for them to obtain their degree as a result of studying. A look at distance students who live near a study centre and have used local support services on a regular basis confirms the importance of degree orientation, especially for the male respondents as 47% of these women and 44% of these men are degree oriented, which is an increase of 7% (women) and 11% (men) compared to the general student population. Put differently, 62% of the degree-oriented women and 58% of the degree-oriented men visited a study centre regularly, while only 52% of the other female students and 40% of the other male students did so.

Students who were seriously working toward a degree used the study centre for reasons such as the following:

'When I prepare for my final examination I would like to have intensive contact [with the study centre] to accompany my work on the thesis (but so far I have not taken any initiatives in this direction).'

'Since I have a full-time job I depend on the competent counselling and tutoring my "mentors" provide in order to achieve my degree.'

Others judge the study centre as very important for their study progress but did not always find the local support they needed:

'In my opinion tutorial support is as important for advanced study and for completing the degree at the FeU as it is in the first- and second-year courses. But unfortunately Munich hardly offers anything at this level! I have a full-time job and therefore cannot "tour Germany" as so many of my fellow students do in order to attend as many tutorials and seminars as possible at other study centres. In addition, subjects which are not compulsory for all students are often not supported by tutorials at all. It would be better if the FeU could spread its local support services more evenly throughout the country so students outside NRW could profit equally from tutorials and seminars!'

The following quote exemplifies why students who study 'just for fun' still may find the study centre useful:

'I have always profited most from tutorial support when it managed, through the use of examples, to connect the knowledge I learned from the course work to its practical application. I suspect that I am not the "typical" distance student. I like my job and am highly motivated to do it well. Studying for a degree at the FeU is a "hobby" I pursue in my free time, purely for my own enjoyment. Nevertheless, I want to use the knowledge gained through my studies later in my work context.'

The findings also support another observation from previous studies, namely that men tend to instrumentalise their study centre visits to a greater extent, weighing the costs of attendance against the expected gains of getting help with their assignments and exam preparation. Women, by contrast tend to make use of local services in order to connect with other students, even if the benefits for their study progress are not immediately apparent. This is not to say that women, who have many demands on their time and energy, are not interested in the benefits to be gained regarding their study progress. But more often than men, these academic factors are interwoven with motivational factors and the support derived from common experiences, as the following quotations show:

'It offers the opportunity to meet other students and to exchange experiences on "distance education".'

'There were at least a few other students studying the same subjects on a similar level so discussions about the subject matter were possible.'

'During the early stages of distance study it is especially important to have contact with other students: it helps in gaining confidence and motivation. Tutors and counsellors need to be aware of the fact that beginners tend to be insecure. During my first year at the FeU I studied micro economics and made an effort to attend the study centre in Munich (at the time there was no underground and the journey was lengthy and complicated as well as unsafe in the dark). But the behaviour of the other students and the mentor in the tutorials so shocked and terrified me that I quit attending after the second time and didn't come back for two years. It was as if they came from another galaxy. Fortunately, the tutor I had when I made a second attempt was super, which is the only reason I attended tutorials more often.'

'Tutorial support was very important for me. In the beginning, the tutorials were the only opportunity for meeting other distance students. Not only did the tutorials help me to understand the subject matter, they also showed me that other students had as much difficulty with the course as I did. Also, I was lucky in that a stable group of students formed after the first three semesters and that this group existed until we completed the degree programme. (I am now in the process of writing my thesis.) Some courses, such as theoretical computer science, I would not have been able to complete successfully without the tutorials. Sometimes, though, I had to attend study centres 75 km or more from my home. But this has almost always been worthwhile.'

'It is important to have someone with whom you can talk over general issues of distance studying or the subject matter of specific courses. Especially for distance students it is very important to have the opportunity to talk subject matter through and not only read it on your own at home.'

'Very important:

Better comprehension of the subject matter.

Studying becomes less of a burden.

Higher motivation through other students.

It is simply easier than sitting at home, alone with your course materials, trying to learn when many questions remain open. In the beginning of my distance studies I lived near a study centre and experienced successes such as passing end-of-term examinations. Now I live a long distance from any study centre. Since I have two children, my time is extremely limited. Studying on my own I lack the motivation.'

'In the study centre it is possible to meet other students. I had the opportunity to ask specific questions concerning the study materials (even if it was not always possible to get answers) and I could measure my own study progress against other students.

For me studying with others meant that I studied much more effectively and I enjoyed participating in the seminars and tutorials.

On balance, attending the study centre was very important for me!'

'During the first years of study, the study centre was (almost) the only opportunity for meeting other students and thus for forming study groups and finding "comrades-in-arms". In a study centre one can ask questionsand learn to discuss the subject matter (!). There is a big difference between writing down the answers to assignments and reporting them orally. Also, fellow students build you up and motivate you and help you measure your study progress.'

'When I first started studying at the FeU I used the study centre frequently because I found great difficulty in knowing how to deal with the study material. The demands are so great that I would never have completed my intermediate examination on my own. I profited most, though, from contact with my fellow students as I was fortunate to become part of a good and effective study group.'

'My friends and acquaintances have only a very hazy idea of distance education and I needed the tutoring/counselling in the study centre to stop me from getting too discouraged. In rural areas distance students are on their own and rely on their study centres to provide basic services, such as help in obtaining secondary materials and literature.'

'The study centre offered the only opportunity to meet the tutors and other students in seminars and tutorials. The study group which my tutor organised and conducted made it possible to study effectively and goal-oriented in preparation for the intermediate examination which I passed successfully. These regular meetings were important for my motivation to continue.'

'Going to the study centre is useful because:

- It makes the structure of the degree programme clearer; it makes it much easier to plan study-related activities; and it is a great help in working through the course materials and assignments or with study problems in general;

- It helps with preparation for written and oral examinations;
- It gives you confidence (because you can join in the discussion) and it makes you feel appreciated (very important as you are otherwise very lonely);
- It provides contact with fellow students and opportunities for exchange.'

'The study centre is a place where you can go in order to clarify questions arising from studying the course material. Also, the contact with other students helps you not to feel quite so "small" and ignorant since you see that others are in danger of being defeated by the same problems. The help of a good tutor (although there are others) is very important and motivating. On the whole I have enjoyed my visits to the study centre, mainly because I was no longer anonymous but had concrete people with whom I could get in touch. My study group also was very important because of its disciplined and goal-oriented work.'

In the comparative study, open-ended answers from both German and British distance students were found to identify:

The following major factors: work pressures, family commitments, and combined pressures from both areas. Both men and women are subjected to pressures through their paid work which often requires long hours, shift work, frequent travelling, or professional changes and new or expanded areas of responsibility. A large proportion of women respondents in both institutions were working full or part time: at the OU 77% of the women compared with 90% of the men, at the FeU 58% of the women compared with 79% of the men.

As with earlier research, the 1996 FeU survey also demonstrates that factors other than geographical access and transport influence students' use of local support services and that these factors have a different impact on women and men studying at a distance. Controlling separately for the extent of paid work and for household composition we find confirmation of the fact that the pressure of family and personal commitments combine to make it extremely difficult for women to fit visits to a study centre into their schedules.

With respect to students' paid work this manifests itself in a response pattern whereby women who hold full-time or part-time jobs with more thanhalf the usual weekly hours (at least 19 hours per week), more often than men in the same employment situations, report frequent visits to a study centre. And while men's attendance rates increase as the extent of their paid work decreases, the opposite is true for women.

The housewife and full-time homemaker obviously have the most problems fitting a visit to the study centre into their days. Thus, there is a tendency for single women to visit study centres more often than women with commitments to a partner and family, while similar patterns do not show in the responses of male, distance students reported. It is fair to conclude that these divergent patterns are based in the gendered division of labour which traditionally leads to an inverse correlation between women's occupational and family commitments.

This can be seen in the reasons given by women distance students for their difficulties in organising study centre attendance, difficulties which frequently arise as a result of their family and domestic responsibilities, sometimes coupled with paid work. Not surprisingly the consequent multiple commitments interfere with the requirements of distance studying, especially when the element of travel to a certain place by a certain time to attend tutorials or participate in group work is involved. For example:

'In my opinion tutoring/counselling is extremely important since without it it's nearly impossible to study effectively and successfully. I have had to relocate frequently and therefore have been to many different study centres which showed great variations with regard to the qualification of the tutors in the subject matter. Another important function of the study centre is the exchange of information between the students (e.g. regarding sending material and information or old exam questions). The weekend seminars are especially effective as are the "qualification weeks" organised by the study centres in northern Germany. Regrettably, none of the study centres I attended offered childcare. This poses a serious problem for women students with children, especially when they have to travel a long distance and the tutorials or seminars start early (usually before 6:00 p.m.).'

'For me the study centre was very important. I would like to attend more often if this were at all possible (time, two small children). Face-to-face seminars or meetings make it easier to learn (less time needed than in studying at home in order to achieve the same learning results). Motivation is greatly increased. It is possible to get insider information (e.g. old exam questions, most frequently covered exam topics).'

'In my view, tutorial support and study centre services (especially computer and Internet access ...) are the most important help for distance students throughout all stages of the degree programme. Because I did not have childcare for my two small children I could only attend infrequently!!'

'I have stopped using the study centre since I cannot organise childcare for my daughter for just a few hours and my child is too young to be left with a childminder for longer periods of time.'

'Even after completing the intermediate examination I am in desperate need of tutorial support. I find it difficult to learn solely from studying the written text, and this presents no less of a problem in the more advanced courses than it did in the introductory materials. Regrettably, there is not much tutorial support for advanced students. Now that I have a child I can no longer afford trips (a 60-minute journey) to NRW (too time-consuming and expensive).'

'As far as tutorial support is concerned Bavaria is a "developing country". Up till now I have had a full-time job. Now that I have a baby I find it nearly impossible to attend tutorials or seminars for exam preparation since hardly anything is offered in Munich and I cannot travel to Nürnberg with my child. (The father cannot breastfeed the baby.) Seriously, too many of the face-to-face seminars the FeU offers take place in northern Germany, and thus are much too expensive. Also, in my opinion, the large number of study centres in North-Rhine Westphalia does not fit the character of a "Fern" (distance) university.'

'I have two small children and therefore often cannot attend because of lack of time. It would be ideal to have tutorials or seminars on a Sunday morning which would have the additional advantage that one is rested. Evening hours are always very inconvenient. Often it is difficult to concentrate. Regrettably, the FeU does not yet offer tutorial support in all subjects. Successful participation also is dependent on the individual tutor.'

'I always had the problem of finding childcare since I was not allowed to bring my children to the study centre. This required a great deal of organisation, even for very short visits.'

'The study centre is too far away (75 km) and as a single mother I have great difficulty getting there (childcare!!).'

'In my view the study centre is very important and I regret that I have no opportunity to visit it. We have three children (4 and 2 years and 14 weeks old). Thus travelling on the train is too difficult, and the study centre does not provide childcare. My studying happens mainly at my desk at home.'

'I did not use the study centre because of the long journey, the lack of atmosphere, the lack of facilities for bringing children, and the scheduling of activities in the evenings which meant that I would have needed a car.'

Some women mentioned the lack of facilities for disabled people, such as provisions for deaf students, or for wheelchair access:

'The nearest study centre is located on the top floor of a building in the city, and there are 150 steps. No elevator which makes it inaccessible for disabled students!'

Since the household, childrearing, and caring responsibilities are regarded mostly as women's work, it comes as no surprise that single women, who can organise their time more freely, visit a study centre more frequently (regular attendance: 55%) than women living with a partner (46%), and that women living in a nuclear family, i.e. mothers with small children have the lowest attendance rate (39%) of all women respondents.

Yet in all three types of similar personal situations, men are less frequent study centre visitors than women, and their attendance rates vary little between the categories. This indicates once again that men are less affected by their commitments to a partner and children and that they are less interested in using the local support services. The gender difference is evidenced especially clearly in the case of single students: only 38% of the single men, but 55% of the single women living near a study centre report regular visits, a difference of 16.2 percentage points.

While the previous sections were concerned with study centre attendance in general, we now look at specific student services available to varying degrees at the FeU study centres. In the 1996 survey we asked students to indicate which of twelve support service items they had used 'often', 'seldom', or 'never' in the course of their first four semesters of distance study. Students were also asked about the relevance of each of these items in relation to their study success by rating it 'very important', 'not very important', or 'totally irrelevant'. Finally, students were asked about the conditions which would have induced them to attend a study centre at all or more frequently.

The basic statistical analysis of the data shows that the most important function of study centres is to help students prepare for examinations and to provide specific advice and tutoring in the concrete subject matter. These services have been used by two-thirds of the respondents and judged as very important by 60% of them. Students who have completed the first phase of their degree programme are more likely to have used these two support offers and to value them more highly than do the less successful students. This may be an indication that study centres can play an important role for study progress. It may also be an indication of the higher commitment of degree-oriented distance students to succeed in their studies and to invest the extra time and money which study centre attendance usually requires.

Students were not only asked about the frequency of their use of study centre services but also about the importance they attached to any given service. The answering patterns show even more clearly that FeU students place the highest value on those local support services which are expected to help them prepare for examinations and on course-related tutorials in their major subject. These were also the most frequented of the events taking place in study centres.

Nearly two-thirds of the respondents considered these items to be very important for their study success (64% and 61%), very few students considered them irrelevant (3.7% and 4.0%). Two other items were also judged important although they were not used as often: tutorials on courses which were not part of the major subject and contact with departmental course team members/teaching staff. These items ranked fourth and sixth in importance but only sixth and eighth in frequency of use. The answering patterns to these questions suggest the existence of intervening factors, although there is a close connection between the frequency of use and the importance a given item has for students' chances of succeeding in their studies.

The gender analysis shows that women use all but one of the study centre services more than their male colleagues, the differences being greatest in regard to tutorials in the major subject and in other subject areas, introductory face-to-face events, exam preparation, and in contacts with teaching staff at the centre. The one item which was frequented more by men is on-line access to the mainframe computer or to the Internet, although both genders used this service only infrequently. Women also place a higher value on each of the study centre services. Of those students who consider a given item very important for their study success, women are more likely than men to avail themselves of the support offered by the institution.

In the 1986 comparative survey, we asked whether visits to the study centre would have been easier if certain conditions had existed. We found similar gender differences in Britain and Germany with regard to provision of childcare, different opening hours or hours for tutorials, and accessibility of the study centre by road or public transport. In all cases, women were more likely to feel that given these conditions attendance would have been easier. This was especially noticeable with respect to childcare provision in the case of mothers of children under fourteen years of age. The fathers of young children, however, tended to feel that this facility would have made no difference to their study centre attendance.

Following up on this, the 1996 FeU survey contained a battery of conditions which students were asked to rate on a five-point scale from, '1 = completely right' to '5 = completely wrong' with regard to their own situation and ability to visit a study centre.

The answers demonstrate a rather pragmatic attitude toward the support services offered in study centres. Students are most inclined to consider attendance if they had more time and if they thought they could ensure their study success by using the service. They also weigh the expected cost and effectiveness and want to be sure that study groups and tutorials or counselling will be immediately useful for their study progress, for doing assignments and for exam preparation. With the exception of the item 'I would have visited a study centre (more often) if it had been necessary for study success', more women affirmed that the conditions listed would have facilitated their use of local support services. The items with the most noticeable gender differences were provision of childcare, again a totally irrelevant consideration for the male respondents, different opening or tutorial times, and better accessibility.

Similar patterns occur when students are asked to state which conditions would have induced them to participate (more frequently) in tutorials or face-to-face seminars, either in the study centre or in a location chosen by the academic department. Students, who were provided with a list of twelve statements with the same five answer categories, were asked to state how well each of the conditions described their own situation. In all cases, more women feel that they could have attended tutorials or seminars if these conditions had existed. The gender differences are greatest with regard to childcare, times of meeting, ease of access, and the wish to have more access to competent advisors on the subject matter.

Students may be motivated to participate in tutorials and seminars by a number of reasons. The 1996 survey therefore included a list of reasons which respondents were asked to rate as 'very important', 'not so important' and 'totally irrelevant' for their decision to attend face-to-face sessions. Once again, the most important function of tutorials and seminars is the direct help students require in order to understand the subject matter and to prepare effectively for their end-of-term examinations. In keeping with the character of such sessions, students are less likely to attend them in order to receive general advice and information.

The answering patterns fit in with results from earlier studies and show that women value all items listed more highly than their male colleagues. With the single exception of the 'contact with teaching staff/course team' (in or from Hagen), there is a higher percentage of women labelling the items listed as very important for their decision to participate. The gender differences range from 8.6 to 19.7 percentage points and are highest with regard to 'more contact with other students' (Ä=19.7%); renewed motivation to continue studying (Ä=19.5%); competent instruction and help in the subject matter (Ä=17.5%); subject-related cooperation with other students (Ä=17.4%); and receiving up-to-date information on the course (Ä=17.1%).

The open-ended answers relating to both the reasons for attending tutorials, seminars and weekend sessions and to deficits in this area, indicate the importance which the women distance students attach to these elements.

They also sum up the general feelings about local support services. The most frequently mentioned aspects have to do with motivation and self-confidence, with isolation and loneliness, with information deficits and difficulties with the subject matter, and lastly with preparing for assignments and examinations. Again, the quotes presented here are only a very small selection of the comments made by women students:

'For me tutoring/counselling and the study centre are both very important. I would not have done as well in my intermediate exam if it had not been for the tutorial support I had. It is extremely important for me to have a specific person to contact when I cannot grasp the course material. Otherwise I would most likely give up too quickly and drop out of the degree programme.'

'I am certain that I would not have completed the first phase of my degree programme without tutorial support. This was extremely important with respect to understanding the subject matter and practising the tests and examinations. The records of previous exams were very helpful in preparing for the intermediate oral examination.'

'The importance of the study centre and tutoring/counselling for me lay in:

- My need as a beginner to learn how to work through written course materials and the specific counselling concerning the structure of my degree programme;
- The opportunity it gave me to control my study progress by comparing myself with other students to see where I stood;
- Exchange with other students;
- Preparation for written and oral examinations;
- And in the continuing renewal of my study motivation.'

'Contacts with tutors and fellow students are absolutely necessary in order to avoid being overwhelmed by feelings of loneliness when sitting alone at one's desk. In the study centre, up-to-date information is always available and help is provided so the students can find their way through the complexities of the degree programme.

Study centres and tutorials connect the students and the university.' 'For me, the exchange with fellow students and the tutorial support from a highly qualified tutor have been very important. Working completely alone, it is impossible to learn how to participate in discussions and how to do presentations!'

'In my view, the exchange with fellow students and tutors about course content is absolutely essential for understanding the subject matter, especially in respect of its relevance and applicability in practice.'

'In my opinion, the study centre is of the greatest importance both as an institution and as an information centre and, especially, as the place providing tutorial support. Regular attendance at tutorials helps me to understand the subject matter of my courses. As a student I can turn to the tutor/counsellor when I have questions concerning course content. Usually these questions are not only answered but placed in the larger context of the subject matter. I am thus enabled to connect the topic in question to a wider range of ideas and subject areas and develop new perspectives leading to a deeper understanding.'

'Both the study centre and the tutoring/counselling are extremely important for distance students:

- Study centres provide help with solving a variety of problems and meeting like-minded others.

Tutoring and counselling serve as psychological supports necessary to complete the course, and provide help with the subject matter. This has a positive effect on the grades one gets in assignments and examinations and motivates the students to participate actively.'

'The study centre and tutoring/counselling have been very important for me during the first study phase, both with respect to mastering the subject matter and for meeting other students, professors and course advisors/ lecturers. In this way distance education was not quite so anonymous, I was not left to cope on my own and had a better chance to master the subject matter.'

'The existence of a study centre in my immediate neighbourhood was the precondition for my decision to register as a distance student. For me it is essential to have opportunities for communication in working through the subject matter and the written course materials, and in the matter of motivation!'

'The most important function of tutoring/counselling for me was the regularity of studying and the content-oriented discussion of different views on the same subject matter. This helped me to form my own opinion on the course topics and to clarify issues which I had not understood. Equally important was the contact with other students in similar circumstances.'

'The tutorial support in a study group was more important than using the facilities of the study centre on my own. During the early stages of my distance studies the tutor/counsellor played an important role in giving me advice when I had difficulties with the subject matter (understanding the course materials) and in suggesting literature. Working in a study group was highly motivating.'

'The study centre is a substitute for a face-to-face university and acts as a bridge between the "single-combat" situation of the individual distance student and the requirements of learning how to work in a team which is essential in today's world.'

'Immensely important. I would have given up long ago if it had not been for the study centre and tutorial support. I probably would not have gone beyond the first two semesters.'

'In my view the study centre and tutoring/counselling are very, very important. Home alone I often lack the motivation to continue studying and would have given up long ago without these support services. In the study centre I meet other students who have similar problems. Together we findthe strength to carry on, to keep on "fighting". Otherwise one often feels left alone, without anywhere to turn in the case of problems. But the study centre and the tutors/counsellors are a great help, something of a "substitute" for a face-to-face university.'

'I use the study centre mainly to photocopy study materials which help me to do the assignments. I attended tutorials in order to meet other students. They also helped me to clarify and structure course contents which were illogical or confusing. It often happened that I only became aware of the importance of a guiding principle or of connections between topics because we covered them in tutorials. Without these services I would not have succeeded in my studies, even though I am very ambitious and highly motivated.'

'During the first phase of my degree programme I participated in a small study group in my major subject of education which was led by a wonderful woman tutor. We met regularly once a month, wrote a term paper together, and finally studied for the intermediate examination together. The group was very important because we motivated each other and because of the support from the tutor. The fact that we were all in similar circumstances (women with children) also had a positive effect.'

'The social aspect of study centre services is very important for me. In order to be able to study I have given up social contact which would arise from other areas of life, such as children in school or involvement in village life. It is therefore very good to meet other people in similar situations through my studies.'

IMPLICATIONS

This is not the first time research on gender issues in distance education has brought to light the differences in the learning styles of women and men. In this chapter of the book I have presented some additional quantitative data and a selection of the many written comments from women in a recent large-scale survey on the uses and relevance of local support services for students of the German FeU. It would not be correct to suggest that all women want to use study centres and can only be successful if they have the chance to learn in face-to-face situations and self-help study groups.

Clearly, this is not the case since the majority of students in Germany, if only for regional reasons; do not have the option of using local support services or connecting with other students.

Others, regardless of gender, may prefer to study on their own, some because this is their individual learning style and some because this is the way they can best organise their lives.

Yet the empirical evidence strongly suggests implications which the existence of gendered learning styles has for DE institutions. This has become clear especially in the comparison of two major DTUs with different provision of local support services. At the OU UK, for instance, first-year students enrolled in foundation courses have traditionally been advised and encouraged to attend weekly tutorials in a nearby study centre and also were required to participate in a compulsory summer school. At the German FeU, where two-thirds of the students are from outside the catchment area of the state in which the university is located and where it can set up study centres on its own initiative, students were expected to study independently, i.e. on their own and with a minimum of institutional support at the local level.

3

The Challenges of a Changing World

During the twentieth century, the United States was a world leader in raising the educational attainment of its population. This important achievement contributed to national productivity growth and extended economic opportunity to formerly disadvantaged groups in society. Now, at the beginning of the twenty-first century, U.S. institutions of higher learning retain an excellent reputation for quality. Less confidence exists, however, in the educational system's ability to meet broad economic and social objectives adequately. This uncertainty stems in part from the shifting global economy and the evolving nature of employment. These doubts also reflect the legacy of widening income inequality over the past quarter century.

These concerns have sparked both federal and state legislation to reform elementary and secondary schooling. The Boston Fed's 47th annual conference brought together experts from a variety of perspectives to analyze current institutional and financial arrangements in the area of education, with the goal of identifying the nature of the shortcomings and appropriate ameliorative actions. Although the primary focus was on the U.S. educational system, the Bank welcomed international perspectives. The experience of other nations provided evidence on the degree to which educational challenges are being driven by changes in the worldwide economy, and offered insights on the strengths and weaknesses of alternative educational systems.

A central theme of the conference was that the U.S. educational system is in the process of being restructured. The key debate is no longer about funding for education. It is about how to change institutions and incentives so as to bring about better educational outcomes. Dissatisfaction with the current education system in the United States was ubiquitous among conference participants. To varying degrees, all claimed that the performance of the average student should be improved, that the educational attainment of low-income and minority students must be raised from currently unacceptable levels, or that greater attention should be placed on developing high-end talent. As a result of their concerns, participants generally welcomed the greater emphasis that public and private officials are placing on improving schools.

Conference participants agreed that education is increasingly important in determining individuals' earnings potential. They also agreed that the total benefits to society from education are greater than the sum of what individuals earn as a result of their increased educational attainment. Participants reached a consensus that these links between personal and social wellbeing and education need to be better communicated to the U.S. populace. Relative to foreign populations, the U.S. population, on average, is highly educated in terms of years of schooling.

However, the average U.S. high school or middle school student does not score highly on international standardized tests. As a response, some participants would concentrate on increasing academic achievement for a given number of years of schooling. Others would focus more on increasing the fraction of the population that completes secondary and higher education, especially since gains in educational attainment have slowed among younger cohorts. Recent education-related reforms in the United States have had two key thrusts. "Standards-based reforms" involve establishing performance benchmarks for students and schools and holding them accountable for their performance. "Choice" involves providing expanded alternatives to traditional public schooling, such as in the form of vouchers and charter schools.

In addition, over the last several decades, states have implemented a variety of changes in school financing in response to voter and legislative actions and judicial decrees. These reforms to school funding formulas are ongoing. In the case of standards-based reforms, two papers presented at the conference point to evidence of likely improvement in academic achievement. Nevertheless, for a variety of technical and philosophical reasons, attendees differed in their assessments of standard-based reforms. Evidence on the efficacy of vouchers and charter schools is still quite limited, given their small scale and relative newness. Finally, on the whole, research indicates that the changes in school funding implemented by various U.S. states have resulted in only limited changes in student performance.

STANDARDS-BASED REFORMS

Conference participants warned policymakers and the public not to declare victory in meeting the challenge of educational reform. Many expressed the view that standards-based policy changes to date represent comparatively small steps, albeit in the right direction. Others warned of possible negative implications from the standards movement. Those who supported the general thrust of standards-based reform pointed to its potential to raise academic achievement. Nevertheless, some adherents of performance benchmarks also cited its inadequacies. Remedies for these problems include raising standards further, refining how test scores are used, or making additional, complementary investments in educational reform.

Participants indicated that, in some states, the new standardized tests either are not rigorous enough to have an effect on student performance or are not sufficiently oriented toward the skills needed to succeed in twenty-first-century labour markets. Furthermore, in most cases, states are not using the information from tests in ways that provide accurate assessments of schools. Teachers often are not receiving information on student test scores in a timely fashion and, in any case, may not have the training or resources to improve their teaching. Participants also advocated for additional institutions to join in the educational reform movement.

These institutions include teachers unions, colleges and universities, and social services providers. Finally, one of the panelists argued that standards-based reforms were more effective when combined with greater choice, which has of yet been only a minor feature of the changes implemented in the United States. All in all, many attendees agreed that countries on th e forefront of standards-based reforms, such as the United States and the United Kingdom, face the ongoing challenge of transforming their educational systems.

Those who appeared more skeptical of the current wave of standards-based reforms were inclined to bring up the tradeoffs associated with any set of incentives. They noted that education encompasses multiple goals, some of which are not reflected in standardized tests. For example, some of the strengths of the U.S. economy-such as an entrepreneurial workforce-can perhaps be traced to aspects of its educational system. Speakers warned that testing efforts run the risk of diverting resources from some sets of students to others, in ways that may not be transparent or desirable.

They also pointed to some conflicts in the incentives created by state educational reforms versus those included in the federal No Child Left Behind legislation. How these differences are resolved will have a bearing on the success of reforms in the United States. Underlying some of the differences of opinion were very different philosophies on the merits of having government-imposed standards for education. One prominent educational reformer noted that educational systems traditionally have been based on implicit standards. He argued that explicit standards are superior because they are more transparent. Educators know what is expected of them, and they can design instructional systems that move toward these goals.

On the other hand, other participants expressed the view that explicit standards were inherently harmful. For example, one member of the audience likened the situation to central planning in the Soviet Union. When steel producers were judged on tonnage, they reduced quality as they increased quantity of production. In this speaker's view, for a variety of markets (including both steel and education), "the only way to make progress is by relying on competitive mechanisms where the customers take their business to the firms with the better products." In the context of the current standards-based reforms, another observer saw perverse repercussions from calls for further research on educational effectiveness. Such investigations could lead to testing "beyond the realm of good policy." He commented, "You don't fatten a pig by weighing it."

THE NEED OR GREATER SUPPORT FOR URBAN SCHOOLCHILDREN

Conference participants agreed that recent efforts to narrow the educational attainment gap between children from wealthy and poor communities have, on the whole, met with limited success. And although the recent interest in standards, accountability, and expanded school choice has been motivated by the view that increased school funding has only limited effects, the presenters advocated a range of policies that arguably would require higher levels of funding for schools in communities with high concentrations of poor and immigrant families. Such schools increasingly are found in large cities.

At a minimum, the solution to educational disparities was said to involve shifting a greater share of overall education funding to elementary and secondary schools in poor areas. However, most of the discussion implicitly seemed to support increased funding for such schools without offsetting reductions in funding for schools in wealthier areas. Participants emphasized that urban schoolchildren face a multitude of problems outside of the schools. They advocated policies that would supplement the services provided during the regular school day (or regular school year) and/or that would expose urban children to environments outside their inner-city neighborhoods.

Moreover, to the extent that the low college attendance rates among students from poor and minority families reflect barriers to financing higher education, the solutions were said to lie either in greater public subsidies for higher education or in greater resources for financial aid.

Conference participants emphasized that education researchers often cannot provide unequivocal answers to what may appear as basic questions to policymakers. Standards and school choice are relatively recent innovations. Some of the effects may not be apparent until these efforts achieve a certain scale. Beyond the inherent difficulty of analyzing new educational structures, conference participants agreed that education research does not yet have definitive answers to underlying questions governing resource allocation such as "How do we produce better-educated individuals?" and "How large are the societal benefits of better education?" For example, conference attendees had an animated discussion of what is more important for disadvantaged children: increasing the quantity or raising the quality of the education they receive. Even those who support "quantity" over may favour different mixes of emphasis among preschool education, summer programs, and access to higher education.

Researchers struggle with even the most basic questions because the process of producing better-educated individuals is complicated, involving student effort, schools, and family and neighborhood influences. Similarly, the production of societal benefits such as improvements in health or reductions in crime also involves a complex mix of inputs, of which schools are only one component. Participants cautioned that research on education must be presented and interpreted in a way that reflects the preliminary state of many of the findings.

This attitude was reflected in both the formal and the informal exchanges. Speakers often disagreed about the magnitudes of the effects of various policies, but they tended to support a blend of approaches to educational reform rather than promoting the exclusive use of a single approach. As testimony to the complexity of educational issues, one veteran attendee of Boston Fed conferences remarked at the conclusion of the conference that this year's speakers seemed more humble and open to discussion than is often the case.

THE HUMAN CAPITAL CENTURY

"American Leadership in the Human Capital Century: Have the Virtues of the Past Become the Vices of the Present? An Address" Claudia Goldin opened the conference by reflecting on educational structures in the "human capital century." The idea that the wealth of a nation is embodied in its people was first voiced in the United States at the beginning of the twentieth century. By the end of the century, the recognition that education is essential for technology adoption and economic growth was universal. Over 100 nations of the world currently provide secondary school enrollment data, and almost all of these countries have higher enrollment rates than the United States did in 1900.

The United States made rapid strides in secondary and higher education in the first half of the twentieth century-despite the arrival of many poor immigrants from other parts of the world. By the mid-1950s, almost 80 percent of 15- to 19-year-olds in the United States were enrolled in school. In contrast, most European nations had general school enrollment rates of less than 30 percent for this age group. Even including the relatively high technical school attendance in Europe, a wide gap existed compared to enrollment rates in the United States.

Goldin argues in her address that the early support for mass secondary education and expanded higher education in the United States was consistent with the economic opportunities of the technologically dynamic, socially open, and geographically mobile New World setting. She identifies various "virtues" of secondary education in the United States that promoted mass education. For example, U.S. secondary schools have been publicly funded and managed by small, fiscally independent districts. Goldin argues that small districts are a virtue because taxpayers who are relatively homogeneous with respect to characteristics such as income, ethnicity, religion, and cultural values are more likely to support education than taxpayers from larger districts (or, as in the case of Europe, nations), where preferences for public goods tend to be more disparate.

Goldin further characterizes twentieth-century U.S. secondary schools as "open and forgiving," secular in control, and gender-neutral. Students could enroll regardless of age, social status, previous school record, religion, or sex, which encouraged school attendance among populations who may have been excluded in a more rigid structure. Finally, relative to the situation in Europe, the curriculum in U.S. secondary schools was "academic yet practical." Students were exposed to a broad base of knowledge that could be applied in a wide variety of occupations. In Europe, by contrast, all but an elite group of youths were channeled into an industrial or specific vocational track that precluded their access to higher education or high-end professions.

Now, at the dawn of the twenty-first century, some of these American education "virtues" are viewed as possible "vices." Popular support for publicly funded alternatives to traditional public education has grown. Indeed, the Supreme Court ruling in Zelman v. Simmons Harris, handed down just one week after the conference, provides further impetus for allowing families to use publicly funded vouchers in private schools. Small, fiscally independent school districts, once seen as a structure that promoted greater spending on education, now are being viewed as a source of serious funding inequities. Educational standards and sanctions for students and schools that do not pass are viewed as potential remedies for the lack of accountability brought on by the open and forgiving systems of the past. Thus, Goldin concludes that an entirely new set of "virtues" could emerge in the twenty-first century.

Yolanda Kodrzycki addresses the links between education and the economy in the conference's first presentation.

Kodrzycki concludes that improving the quality of U.S. education should be of rising concern. In addition, as racial and ethnic minority groups account for a growing share of the U.S. population, improving their educational opportunities goes hand-in-hand with overall economic growth objectives. Examining the U.S. evidence, Kodrzycki shows that overall high school and college completion rates have risen considerably since 1970, but that progress among younger cohorts has slowed.

Although the United States has the highest international ranking for average number of years of schooling completed, average scores on standardized tests administered to secondary school students are not in the top half of the international distribution and have not improved in recent years. Kodrzycki interprets these test score findings as evidence of mediocre quality of schooling for the typical U.S. student and predicts that the lack of improvement in education could constrain productivity growth in coming decades.

The educational attainment of minority groups is of increasing importance because their share of the population is rising. The most dramatic population increase has been among Hispanics, who now constitute over 15 percent of young adults, compared to only 5 percent three decades ago. Among young adults, the gap between black and white high school completion rates has been closed, but a large gap continues to exist in college completion rates. School completion rates among Hispanics lag far behind for both high school and college, owing in part to large numbers of recent immigrants. Furthermore, at comparable levels of education, black and Hispanic minorities perform worse by various measures and have fewer classroom resources than whites.

Kodrzycki performs simulation exercises to determine how much of the gap in earnings between whites and minority groups are due to educational differences. She finds that, for full-time male earners, one-fifth to one-third of the earnings gap is due to minority groups' having fewer years of schooling than whites. For females, the deficit in the amount of schooling accounts for roughly one-half of the earnings gap. The remainder of the observed wage gaps for full-time earners is attributable to minorities' earning less than whites for comparable years of education. On the basis of the evidence concerning indicators such as test scores, computer and Internet access, and literacy, Kodrzycki concludes that the lower earnings reflect the fact that blacks and Hispanics receive lower quality education than whites-or, at least, that the education they receive does not make up for any deficiencies arising from family resources and neighborhood influences.

Finally, Kodrzycki examines the evidence on shortfalls of talent in scientific and technical fields. These concerns emerge periodically because the demand for workers trained in engineering, information technology, and similar occupations tends to spike upward abruptly in response to changes in technology or government policies. The supply of such workers inevitably responds with a lag, given the length of time required for education and training, causing a temporary shortage. Looking ahead to the coming decades, projections for only modest growth in the number of college graduates in the United States imply some constraints in filling positions, even if students respond to market signals when choosing their college major. Thus, Kodrzycki concludes that mechanisms to retrain the adult workforce appear to deserve greater attention than in the past.

In his discussion of Kodrzychi's paper, Lawrence Katz notes that the slow growth in the supply of college-equivalent workers in the United States during the last two decades stands in sharp contrast to the increases earlier in the twentieth century and has had a major impact on wage inequality. Other countries with decelerations in the rate of educational advance in recent decades-such as the United Kingdom and Canada-also have experienced substantial increases in educational wage differentials. By contrast, countries with continued rapid expansion in educational attainment-France, the Netherlands, and Germany-have not.

Students from lower-income and minority families account for much of the slowdown in U.S. College enrollment and completion rates, and these types of families increasingly are located in inner cities. Katz suggests that programs to assist low-income and minority families in moving to other locations with higher school quality, greater safety from crime, and supervised after-school activities should be considered important complements to educational policies that are designed to improve human capital development.

Finally, Katz addresses Kodrzycki's simulation results showing that the preponderance of black-white wage differentials occurs within education groups. He cautions that this finding does not imply lower returns to education for minorities than for whites. Instead, it largely reflects developmental deficits associated with differential family, neighborhood, and school resources, as well as lingering racial stigma and labour market discrimination. Katz views policies to raise the quantity of schooling received by minorities as the single most important lever for improving their economic status.

The second discussant, Paulo Renato Souza, addresses education in economic development, focusing on the example of Brazil, where he serves as Minister of Education. From 1900 until 1975, Brazil's rate of economic growth was second only to Japan's. Yet, despite enjoying the reputation of having the best higher education system in Latin America, Brazil had very high illiteracy and dropout rates, especially in the poorest sections of the country and among blacks. With the growing importance of knowledge as the basis of economic growth in the latter part of the twentieth century, Brazil determined that it could no longer base its economic policies on abundant natural resources and cheap, uneducated labour. The nation now recognizes that if it is to maximize economic growth, its education system must promote the ability to learn and must provide its citizens with opportunities for lifelong learning.

To further this goal, during the 1990s, the national government of Brazil implemented the Bolsa-Escolaf card, which provides grants to low-income families whose children are enrolled in school. The Brazilian government also revamped curriculums and the system for evaluating schools.

Between 1994 and 2000, the overall elementary school enrollment rate increased from 87 percent to 96 percent, and the differentials by income and racial group narrowed significantly. The percentage of students repeating grades fell, allowing greater percentages to pursue secondary education before entering the workforce. In the discussion period, it was noted that Mexico has successfully implemented a program similar to the Brazilian Bolsa-Escola card to boost attendance among poor students in rural areas.

Determining the appropriate level of investment in education requires going beyond the earnings effects that have been the traditional focus of economics literature. Accordingly, Barbara Wolfe and Robert Haveman catalog and estimate the social returns to education. For example, greater parental education is associated with greater education for children and improved health of children. People with more education tend to make more efficient consumer choices, devote more resources to charitable giving, and commit less crime. Economists have used a variety of techniques to isolate the effects of schooling on labour market earnings, independent of additional compounding factors such as a student's ability, drive, or family influences.

The consensus from this research is that an added year of education yields a rate of return between 7 percent and 9 percent. Adding in the full range of benefits from education, Wolfe and Haveman estimate that the total social returns may be double the conventional estimates. Their conclusion implies that investments in education should be increased from current levels.

The added social returns analyzed by Wolfe and Haveman fall into either or both of two categories. Private nonmarket returns are the nonmonetary benefits that families receive from education, and externalities are the benefits received by others in society. These types of benefits are not directly valued in the marketplace. To arrive at estimates, Wolfe and Haveman appeal to the economic theory that people combine efficient mixes of "inputs" (such as financial resources, education, and so forth) in achieving desired "outcomes" (such as, for example, improved health status for oneself or one's children, or increased education for one's children).

The authors then estimate the implicit marginal value of schooling by drawing on empirical studies measuring how "productive" a dollar of financial resources and a year of education are in achieving different social outcomes. On the basis of the existing literature, which encompasses only some of the nonmarket returns and externalities cataloged in their paper, Wolfe and Haveman conclude that the total social returns to schooling may be as great as 14 percent to 18 percent.

Wolfe and Haveman observe that developed countries tend to devote about 5 percent to 7 percent of their GDP to education, including both private and government spending as well as the foregone earnings of college and university students. Since few other investments seem able to claim returns as large as their estimates for education, the share of societal resources devoted to education should likely be increased. Wolfe and Haveman caution, however, that their research does not indicate how the extra spending should be allocated between the private and public sectors.

To reach such a conclusion requires determining what share of the benefits individuals receives, versus how much constitutes an externality received by society at large. It also requires forming a judgment on the need for government intervention to alleviate the constraints lower-income families face in paying for education. The discussants agreed that investments in education should be guided by comprehensive measures of the returns and that the total social returns to education exceed the labour market returns that have been the traditional focus of economic studies. Each focused his remarks on ways to improve the measurement of social returns and endorsed the need for a next generation of research along these lines.

As an introduction to his discussion, Daron Acemoglu raises two key questions related to determining the appropriate level of investment in education. First, based on the external returns to education, should governments intervene more in this sector than we observe today? Second, has the overall societal return to education increased over time, mirroring the trend in private pecuniary returns? Acemoglu concludes that these questions have not yet been adequately answered. Acemoglu points out that the studies employed by Wolfe and Haveman are based on the ordinary least squares (OLS) methodology and, therefore, do not establish the true causal link between education and outcomes.

Individuals who obtain relatively high levels of education differ in their family and social background from individuals who receive less education, and these background variables likely contribute to their observed choices of what to consume, where to live, how to raise their families, and so forth. It is misleading, he says, to attribute all of the observed differences to their higher levels of education. Acemoglu illustrates the importance of methodology by using an example from his own research of the spillovers from education in local labour markets. Studies using the OLS methodology conclude that the average worker is more productive, and is therefore paid more, in locations with a high concentration of highly educated workers.

The implication is that the presence of these educated workers has beneficial effects on the working population at large, such as through more pervasive adoption of technologies and organizational arrangements that enhance productivity. However, when Acemoglu applies instrumental variable techniques to the same question, he finds that the spillover effects in local labour markets from highly educated workers to other workers are minimal at best. Acemoglu acknowledges that his findings on local labour markets do not preclude the importance of other social benefits from education. For example, recent research using appropriate instrumental variable methodology finds that individuals who obtain more education, because compulsory schooling laws preclude them from dropping out of school, are less likely to commit crime.

Paul Schultz also focuses on methodological issues in his discussion. A technical assumption underlying Wolfe and Haveman's approach is that more highly educated individuals are more efficient in producing outcomes, but that they do not differ from less-educated individuals in the "production techniques" they employ. Schultz cites a seminal study on agriculture showing that more-educated farmers are more productive, in part, because they use different production techniques from those used by less-educated farmers.

Schultz argues that similar mechanisms may be at work in the child-rearing context. More-educated mothers may manage to produce healthier children by substituting other inputs for their time. In computing the social benefits of mothers' education, one must subtract the cost of these added inputs. More generally, Schultz calls for deeper research into the technology of production of nonmarket goods: How do educated parents allocate their time? What activities benefit and suffer as a result?

Thomas Downes reviews the evidence on how state and local financing reforms have affected educational quality. His study encompasses three sets of reforms: court-mandated changes in the allocation of state aid to local school districts; voter-imposed limitations on local taxes used for education; and state funding of alternative educational institutions, such as charter schools. On the whole, these reforms have served to increase the states' share of elementary and secondary school funding and may, therefore, have provided more equal funding across school districts within states.

Downes concludes that finance reforms implemented in response to court orders seem to have little, if any, impact on the distribution of student performance. Tax and expenditure limits appear to be associated with some decline in average mathematics scores and (at least in one study) an increase in dropout rates, but he finds no discernible changes in the distribution of student performance across school districts.

Compared to the evidence on other finance reforms, the literature on charter schools remains quite limited because they account for only about 1 percent of total student enrollment nationwide. Students attending charter schools have been found to experience an initial, temporary decline in test scores, which is consistent with the general findings on students who change schools. The presence of charter schools does not appear to change the performance of students in traditional schools, although some evidence suggests that charter schools have a positive effect when they provide a threshold level of competition. Because the effects of charter schools seem to be different, depending on how long they are in operation and how large a share of the local school market they account for, Downes concludes that the long-run effects of competition have yet to be evaluated.

In reviewing the school finance literature, Downes distinguishes between two strands of research: studies of reforms in particular states and national comparisons of generic (or "canonical") reforms. Downes observes that each type of research has idiosyncratic strengths and weaknesses. For example, policymakers interested in the effects of reforms in California would benefit from studying the consequences of the restrictions on local funding of education that have grown out of the 1976 Serrano v. Priest court case and the results of the limitations on property taxation and per-pupil spending imposed by the 1978 passage of Proposition 13. Because of unique circumstances about both the reforms and the economy in California, however, the conclusions would not necessarily provide useful indicators for other states.

On the other hand, comparisons of student test performance in states that had and had not undergone finance reforms could provide estimates of the average impacts of such categories of reforms, but sh ould not be construed as evaluating exactly the same policy changes in each state. Downes concludes that state-level and national-level analyses should be used in concert to guide policymakers.

Both discussants express the view that, to date, the research on school funding has fallen short of what policymakers need. Julian Betts prefaces his remarks by emphasizing the difficulty of drawing definitive conclusions about what causes educational outcomes. While disparities in school finances may matter, so do disparities in home and neighborhood environments, as well as hard-to-capture differences among school districts-such as the quality of local school administrators and the attitudes of local residents. In his view, these other factors remain influential, whatever equalization may occur as a result of fiscal reforms.

Betts argues that even careful econometric studies may mistakenly attribute changes in student achievement to changes in the financial support for schools, while ignoring simultaneous developments that differ across states or school districts. For example, concern about poor student achievement may lead both to lawsuits that result in changes in financial resources and to increased parental involvement in the schools. A similar problem exists in trying to assess the impact of charter schools: Concern about student achievement that leads to the establishment of more charter schools may also lead to the hiring of reform-minded administrators who take steps to improve all public schools. Whatever change occurs in public school student achievement should not be attributed only to competition from charter schools. Because state-level analyses inevitably fail to capture some relevant details, Betts recommends further pursuit of district-level studies.

Michael Rebell provides a context for his remarks by observing that suburbanization in post-World War II America brought increased economic segregation, leading to unprecedented disparities in financial resources across school districts. As dramatized three decades ago in the U.S. Supreme Court case of Rodriguez v. San Antonio Independent School District, poor school districts could fall far short of matching the school funding provided by nearby wealthy school districts, even if they were willing to levy relatively high property tax rates. Since the Rodriguez decision held that the federal courts could not provide a remedy, school-funding cases have fallen to individual state courts.

Rebell interprets the economics literature reviewed by Downes as saying that "money doesn't matter," since, on average, states that were subject to court decrees on school financing did not show any convergence in the academic performance of students from rich and poor districts. He finds this conclusion unhelpful, if not misleading. In many states, court orders had limited implications. In some cases, they were ignored by state legislatures, while in other cases; they pertained only to certain forms of education spending. The national studies performed to date fail to distinguish between such circumstances. A more useful approach, according to Rebell, is to perform comparative case studies of individual states.

This methodology would likely uncover legal strategies that are effective in bringing about equalization of educational resources and performance. On the whole, the session on educational funding appeared to result in participants reaching two different conclusions. Those inclined to believe that "money must matter" called for further study of how to allocate school budgets more efficiently. For example, what is known about the efficacy of lengthening the school year or of alternative ways of investing in professional development for teachers? Others more inclined to believe "money doesn't matter much" voiced support for experimenting with standards-based reforms or school choice.

In his address, Michael Barber provides perspectives on education reforms in the United Kingdom, which he has overseen on behalf of the Blair government. Since the late 1980s, the United Kingdom has put in place a framework for continuous improvement of education. Many of the measures are similar to reforms in the United States. The U.K. framework includes setting high standards through a national curriculum and school inspections, substantial budget allocation authority for individual schools, readily available data to enable schools to compare their own performance against those of other schools, and expanded investments in instructors' professional development.

Signs of success to date include rising scores on international standardized mathematics and literacy tests, such as the Program for International Student Assessment (PISA). However, the Blair government remains cognizant of a long list of remaining challenges. These include making better progress at the secondary school level (such as lowering dropout rates and creating more effective vocational education programs and links to out-of-school learning opportunities), offering higher quality programs for the most-talented students, increasing access to university education for students from lower socioeconomic groups, and developing the leadership talent of head teachers.

Barber draws an analogy between the ongoing efforts at education reform and the mission of explorers Lewis and Clark in the early 1800s to discover a route from the East Coast to the West Coast of the United States. In Barber's words: "I feel as though we've reached Kentucky, but we don't know what's beyond the Mississippi." The remainder of Barber's remarks addresses his longer-term vision for transforming the educational system of the United Kingdom.

In Barber's mind, the transformation of the education system must be directed at achieving two goals simultaneously: having the most talented workforce possible and improving the equity of educational outcomes. Essential in this process is moving to a system of informed professional judgment, whereby teachers have access to high quality data on student performance and teaching practices, and where their teaching is driven by what these data tell them. Under such a system, the process of teaching would be re-engineered, with time reallocated toward activities such as professional growth, planning, and mentoring. Schools might choose to be combined into flexible networks that share innovations and services with one another. Educational outcomes would be transparent to taxpayers, to students, and to their families. Moreover, as schools become genuinely responsive to the learning needs and aspirations of individual pupils and their families, Barber envisions less need for the kinds of formal accountability system s that are currently being developed.

Eric Hanushek and Margaret Raymond evaluate the U.S. experience in setting up accountability systems for schools and school districts. As the authors point out, as of 1996, only 10 states had active accountability systems, while by 2000, just 13 states had yet to introduce such systems. Under the federal No Child Left Behind Act of 2001, all states must move in this direction. Hanushek and Raymond review the diversity of accountability systems across states and explore their incentive effects.

The authors express concern that state performance benchmarks often emphasize process and input measures that are relatively easy to change but that have been found to bear little relationship to student achievement. Even when states use performance benchmarks such as standardized test scores, which Hanushek and Raymond claim are closely linked to student achievement, states tend to report the results in ways that prevent an accurate assessment of how well or poorly schools are performing. States most commonly issue what Hanushek and Raymond refer to as "status change measures."

For example, such measures indicate the change in the average test score for a particular grade in a particular school or school district from one year to another. The problem with this approach is that the students in, say, third grade in one year are different from the students in third grade the next year. Improvement in average scores may simply reflect a better draw of students (from more advantaged backgrounds, for example), rather than any overall improvement in schooling. A superior approach, they argue, would involve tracking individual students over time and aggregating these year-by-year changes into an overall summary for the school or school district. Only four states currently adopt this approach, which is much more demanding from the perspective of data requirements.

Some previous studies referenced by Hanushek and Raymond examine changes in student performance and other outcomes after individual states introduced accountability systems. Hanushek and Raymond present the first-ever attempt at measuring whether states that introduce accountability systems show more marked improvement in student performance than those that do not. Using National Assessment of Educational Progress (NAEP) mathematics scores for two student cohorts in the 1990s, the authors find that the presence of some form of accountability is associated with an increase in state NAEP scores. They also find some, albeit weak, support for the view that states that merely issue "report cards" on schools see less increase in student test scores than states with a system that has some form of reward (sanction) for good (poor) performance.

Some critics of state-standardized testing argue that it provides incentives to place greater numbers of students into special education programs so as to exclude them from the tests and thereby boost reported average scores. To the contrary, Hanushek and Raymond provide statistical evidence that although states introducing standardized testing did increase special education placements, these increases were not out of line with the nationwide trend during the 1990s. In his commentary, Peter Dolton argues that designing incentives to achieve education goals is inherently difficult. For one thing, education encompasses multiple goals-not just achieving higher test scores.

If educators are expected to devote effort to important but hard-to-measure goals-such as fostering the emotional growth of children and preparing them for their eventual social responsibilities-then the incentives to achieve measurable goals must be weakened. Another issue is that teachers are responsible to multiple stakeholders-including school heads, education authorities, parents, taxpayers, and others. To the extent these groups have competing objectives, the incentives teachers face with the introduction of an accountability system are inevitably weakened.

Dolton argues that the conditions needed for accountability systems to provide an efficient allocation of educational resources do not square with reality. In particular, effective accountability requires that all the consumers of education have the power to influence educational priorities as well as the means to choose alternative providers of education in a competitive environment. What happens, Dolton asks, if the voices of more affluent and more highly educated parents prevail over those of other "consumers"? What happens if these influential parents choose to exit the public school system in favour of private schools, rather than continuing to voice their concerns?

Although the introduction of greater accountability has been associated with improvements in standardized test scores in both the United States and the United Kingdom, Dolton argues that little if anything is known about its other possible effects. For example, does accountability result in greater expenditure of public or family resources? Does it result in school resources being reallocated away from top- and bottom-performing students, and more toward those students who are at the threshold of passing the tests? Does accountability ultimately result in less progress in meeting long-term objectives, such as a better citizenry or a labour force with more transferable skills?

Thomas Kane emphasizes that school test scores provide imprecise signals about how well schools are performing in a given year. Scores can be affected by transient events, such as poor classroom chemistry in a given year or a school-wide disruption on the day of the test. As a consequence, average school test scores exhibit relatively weak correlation from year to year, especially in the case of small schools. The problem of imprecision becomes even worse when states base their evaluations on changes in performance over time. Furthermore, the variation in scores across schools is much smaller than variation across students within schools, casting doubt on the advisability of interpreting test scores as measures of how well or poorly different schools are performing.

Given the inherent imprecision in measuring performance, some commentators have questioned whether state accountability systems might err in rewarding high-ranking schools too much. Kane provides evidence to the contrary In California, which has a relatively generous award system for schools and faculty that achieve improvement in test-score performance, the awards are at most only one-tenth of the payoff the students can expect to receive in the labour market as a result of greater learning. Thus, in a sense, the inexactness of test scores is already taken into account in establishing only small incentives for educators.

On the other hand, Kane expresses concerns about possible inconsistencies between existing state accountability standards and those being introduced by the No Child Left Behind Act. States tend to sanction or reward schools based on changes in performance over time, but under the federal legislation, schools will face sanctions if any racial or ethnic subgroups within the school fail to meet certain proficiency levels. Finally, Kane warns that using the NAEP tests to study the impact of state accountability standards is problematic for the 1990s because the reported scores exclude students whose disabilities resulted in accommodations while taking the test, such as extra time or having test questions read to them. The proportion of students granted accommodations increased after the Individuals with Disabilities Act of 1996, and Kane cites the cases of two states with prominent accountability systems that also had large increases in exclusion rates.

The majority of U.S. states now has or is phasing in examinations that students must pass in order to graduate from high school. Examples mentioned at the conference include the MCAS (Massachusetts Comprehensive Assessment System) and the FCAT (Florida Comprehensive Assessment Test). John Bishop's paper analyzes the likely effects of these new exams, based on evidence from longer-standing testing programs that he calls curriculum-based external exit exam (CBEEE) systems. These examinations evaluate students' mastery of the high school curriculum, and individual-student scores play a role in determining university admission. In the United States, the primary example is the Regents Exam in New York. Such examinations are more prevalent in other countries.

Where they are found, both the new graduation tests in the United States and the longer-standing CBEEEs cover all or almost all high school students, define achievement relative to an absolute standard, vary according to the curriculum in a specific geographical area (such as a state, province, or country), and are controlled by the same education authority that designs the curriculum and funds elementary and secondary education. In addition, both types of examinations have consequences for students and schools, although CBEEEs generally have been more oriented toward measuring student achievement rather than determining who graduates.

In four separate samples, Bishop finds that the existence of CBEEE systems improves academic performance substantially-one-half to two-thirds of a grade level equivalent. He measures performance according to scores on widely applied standardized tests that are not curriculum-based, and, using regression analysis, compares these scores in areas with and without CBEEEs. The four test measures are the national average performance of eighth graders on the Third International Math and Science Study (TIMSS); national average performance of 15-year-olds in the Program for International Student Assessment (PISA); the Canadian province average performance of 13-year-olds on the International Assessment of Educational Progress (IAEP); and New York versus other states' average high school student performance on the Scholastic Achievement Test (SAT).

Bishop hypothesizes that CBEEEs increase achievement through various positive incentives for students, parents, teachers, and school administrators. He argues that such tests provide an offset to the problem of peer pressure against studying. Teachers no longer act as judges of their students' performance, but in effect become coaches for their students, helping them pass exams that are established by an authority outside the classroom. The Canadian study was supplemented by additional data showing that schools in provinces with CBEEEs scheduled more hours of math and science instruction and assigned more homework. Students in these provinces reported spending more time reading for pleasure and devoted a greater share of television-viewing time to educational programs.

While Bishop expects the new high school exams in the United States to have some of the same effects as CBEEEs, he notes some crucial differences. The new exams set minimum competencies for graduation. Thus, if anything, they are likely to result in more class time being devoted to practicing low-level skills, as opposed to inducing teachers to spend more time on cognitively demanding skills. Furthermore, if only a pass-fall signal is generated by the exams, and if passing is necessary to graduate, Bishop argues that standards are likely to be set low enough to allow almost everyone to pass the test after multiple tries. Thus, these exams are not likely to spur the great bulk of students to increase their effort.

In commenting on Bishop's paper, David Figlio expresses support for the view that higher standards can improve student performance. He notes that Bishop's findings are complementary to other research that finds that students learn more and behave better when they have a teacher with high grading standards. However, Figlio is skeptical that the introduction of comprehensive, curriculum-based tests can increase student performance as much as Bishop finds. Figlio argues that some reverse causality is at work in Bishop's study.

For example, the fact that children in provinces with CBEEEs read more for pleasure and devote a greater share of their television-viewing time to educational programs may be attributes of their communities rather than outcomes of the CBEEEs. Parents in provinces imposing CBEEEs are likely to have a greater preference for certain types of instruction than parents living elsewhere, and these tastes result in both a difference in curricular emphasis and in setting standards. To attribute the full difference in test scores to the CBEEEs-and none to parental preferences-overstates the role of these exams.

Figlio calls for more research on the distributional consequences of testing. For example, although Bishop argues that CBEEEs induce students to work harder, it is also plausible that they may discourage low achievers, causing them to drop out in greater numbers. Finally, Figlio expresses concern about the simultaneous existence of school standards and student standards. The No Child Left Behind law removes federal education aid from "failing" schools. The threat of such a penalty may inhibit states from identifying schools as poor performers. Figlio suggests that the federal legislation may have been a factor in causing Florida to delay implementation of higher standards for its comprehensive assessment test.

Citing separate research showing that student performance is lower in schools that give merit pay to all or most teachers (regardless of individual teacher productivity) than it is in schools with no merit pay, Figlio speculates that imposing low student standards might be worse than having none at all. Ellen Guiney warns that educational reformers need to create a coherent system in order to improve instruction in urban classrooms, where students tend to exhibit the greatest learning deficiencies. As currently implemented, standards-based reforms rest on assumptions that do not hold in large school districts. Virtually no large district provides timely information to school principals and teachers about what individual students are and are not learning.

Timeliness is particularly critical in the urban environment, since students change schools frequently. Furthermore, low-achieving students have little confidence that schooling has value for them, since their own experience is largely contradictory. Guiney argues that teachers often do not know how to assess individual student progress or how to design an appropriate course of study based on individual need. This problem is acute in urban schools, where teachers fear losing control of the classroom and, therefore, engage in little discourse with their students.

Teachers are not evaluated on the basis of how their students perform on curriculum-based exit examinations, which weakens the incentive to improve instruction. Moreover, even if incumbent teachers were found to be poor performers, a supply of other, well-prepared instructors ready and willing to step into urban education does not exist. Finally, urban schools and school systems lack information on how to organize financial and human resources so as to improve instruction. More research, and more dissemination of such research, is necessary.

The concluding panel focused on policies to improve educational outcomes. Chester Finn outlines four "theories of action" that have driven educational reforms and assesses their relative strengths and weaknesses. The first two approaches operate chiefly within the framework of familiar institutional arrangements. One theory is that school authorities are committed to improving educational outcomes and have the expertise to do so. The appropriate action in this case would be to provide additional resources to the existing educational system.

This would likely lead to changes such as smaller class sizes, longer school days, introduction of new textbooks, and added use of technology. Finn believes such a policy works only in the case of unusually high-quality leadership within the school system. A second theory holds that school officials are motivated to improve but need further training on effective organization and teaching methods. The policy response in this case would be added involvement of outside educat ion experts. Finn views outside professional experts as a useful adjunct to educational reform, but he does not believe they can be entrusted with the responsibility of making reform happen.

Finn's remaining two theories of action view outsiders as the drivers of education reform. Government-driven reform is premised on a greater need for higher levels of government to be involved in elementary and secondary education. For example, the No Child Left Behind Act calls for state governments, backed by the federal government, to develop educational standards, test performance against these standards, and institute a set of incentives to ensure positive results. An alternative view is that educational reform should harness the power of market forces by introducing competition among schools and providing families a choice of schools. Unlike the other theories of action, Finn notes that market-driven reforms have not yet been tried on a large scale.

Finn argues that government-driven and market-driven reforms are useful complements. The market-driven approach, by itself, lacks informed consumers. This problem can be obviated by the introduction of government standards and testing. On the other hand, while a government-driven accountability system is good at identifying failing schools, Finn argues that market-oriented alternatives (such as charter schools) are much more effective in implementing corrective actions. The second panelist, Alan Merten, emphasizes that some of the same forces influencing reform in primary and secondary schools are also affecting higher education.

As a result of broader access to post-secondary education, the typical university student in the United States is no longer between the ages of 18 and 22 years, enrolled full time, and living on campus. Therefore, the structure of learning must be reformed. Courses of fixed duration with grades from failing to excellent make less sense than before. Thus, universities are beginning to adopt the model that the "time and place" of learning are variable, but that minimum standards must be set for knowledge gains. In addition, Merten argues that educational leaders at the post-secondary level must become more willing to take risks, measure the relevant outcomes, become more effective managers of resources, and learn from failures.

Merten observes that, in their quest for accountability and cost-cutting, public officials have become less supportive of education. He urges education leaders at all levels to become more aggressive not only in managing resources more efficiently, but in making the case for the allocation of more adequate resources for education. This requires clarifying the link between education and economic and social prosperity. He notes that the U.S. educational system has been instrumental in expanding opportunities for women, ethnic minorities, and non-U.S. citizens. Further progress is needed in light of the continuing need to develop a workforce for the information economy. Unfortunately, Merten notes, the terrorist attacks of September 11, 2001, have engendered some moves to restrict access of foreigners to U.S. higher education institutions.

Finally, Merten lists three features that distinguish higher education markets in the United States. These are intense competition among providers of education, merit-based pay, and compensation that differs according to academic discipline and area of expertise. Given the excellent worldwide reputation of this nation's universities, Merten urges public policymakers to assess whether these structures may usefully be adopted at lower levels of education. Panelist Richard Murnane argues that unless public officials, teachers unions, business groups, and the community at large band together to support reform of urban public schools, we are likely to see ever-increasing diversion of public resources to alternative schools, with the possible demise of public schools "as we have known them."

As a first step, effective school reform must encompass the development of measures of student outcomes that are meaningful in the context of current labour markets. To earn a decent living, workers must increasingly engage in nonroutine problem solving and in communicating the meaning of information. Tests that are geared only toward measuring students' reading comprehension and their ability to perform computations are not adequate in achieving effective reform. Only selected state testing programs currently go beyond these outdated standards.

Murnane argues that school reform must also encompass efficient analysis of individual student performance and the training of teachers to improve student outcomes. Otherwise, the information provided, even in good testing programs, will not be put to its desired use. Beyond such reforms within the traditional schooling context, Murnane calls for added resources to support summer learning programs for low-income children, so as to prevent them from falling behind their higher-income peers during the periods when they are not enrolled in school.

Murnane draws lessons from the experiences to date with alternative schools. Charter and voucher schools have been reluctant to accept students with disabilities, students whose first language is not English, disruptive students, and students who change schools frequently. Policymakers should interpret their reluctance as evidence that current funding formulas do not compensate schools adequately for educating these categories of students. Murnane urges the creation of a level playing field on which traditional public schools compete with charter schools and voucher schools.

Experiments with alternative schools also offer examples of resource use that could be applied in traditional public school settings if certain institutional rules were made more flexible. As an example, Murnane cites Boston's experience with pilot schools, which are staffed by personnel who have agreed to waive certain elements of teacher union work rules in exchange for greater flexibility in designing and implementing instructional programs. That these schools are attracting talented teachers and pursuing innovative educational programs is a testament to their success.

The final panelist, Warren Simmons, notes that the No Child Left Behind legislation has set education goals for 2014 that are far more ambitious than those contained in prior versions of standards-based reforms. Like these earlier efforts, Simmons believes the current moves are doomed to fall short of their goals unless standards and assessments are integrated into the other aspects of education policy, such as professional development, curriculum development, school funding, public engagement, and school organization. Simmons argues that large gaps continue to exist between our current levels of educational attainment and our desired levels.

The existing educational system has been effective, at most, in moving elementary and middle school students from substandard to basic levels of achievement. It has not been effective in raising children's performance to proficient levels, in making progress in high schools, or in closing the gap between white students and minorities-particularly African-Americans and Hispanics. Simmons emphasizes that instead of continuing to focus on individual school performance, reform should concentrate on systemic improvement in the education system. This requires developing an education leadership made up of experts from different disciplines and sectors that are committed to working toward a common agenda. Whatever is learned at a national level must be customized for local school districts by local organizations.

The local efforts must involve agencies and organizations outside the schools who are effective in communicating to the public about education reform. They must also involve groups such as social services providers and juvenile justice officials who deal with related issues. In the general discussion period, Simmons gave examples of ways in which state evaluation criteria for teachers, textbook purchasing decisions, and the curriculum at a major local teacher college did not keep pace with changing educational standards set by the Philadelphia school system, hampering their successfu l implementation.

4

Hybrid Socio-Constructivist Model

This chapter evaluates a socio-constructivist hybrid model for training K-12 teachers in Brazil in the use of Informatics in education. The method applied combines both face-to-face exchanges and a WEB-based distance approach made possible by Internet technology. The characteristics of such training and its main objectives are analyzed according to the collected data presented. The main conclusions reached by this research are presented, especially those addressing the importance of care and coherence for knowledge creation in a socio-constructivist training model developed with the help of the Internet. Comparisons between this model and the traditional model are also presented.

A cost-effectiveness analysis of socio-constructivist training is carried out and conclusions regarding the outcome derived from this adopted paradigm are developed. Finally, some recommendations are made to enhance this highly innovative methodology for training K-12 teachers in the use of Information and Communication Technologies (ICT) in their classrooms. In 1997, the Brazilian Ministry of Education and Culture (MEC) defined and launched a national public policy for the use of Informatics in Brazilian K-12 public schools, by means of a broad-based Program involving all 27 Brazilian States, known as Projects of Informatics in Education (PROINFO). While the Federal Government is in charge of investing in equipment and teacher training, the Brazilian states have autonomy to implement their PROINFO, as they think fit.

PROINFO-The National Program of Informatics in Education-aims to initiate the public educational system into the process of using state-of-the-art technology in the classroom, as well as to train human resources to develop their work adequately. To accomplish this target, PROINFO along with the acquisition and deployment of the necessary equipment, has stressed the need for training the teachers, using partnerships with universities as training agents. Hence, together with state and municipal governments, Nucleos de Tecnologia Educacional (NTEs) were created to work as hubs of teacher training. NTEs are decentralized structures to promote the dissemination of Informatics within the pedagogical practice in public schools in each state.

In these hubs, there are multipliers (teacher trainers) with qualifications (more than 360 course hours) in Informatics in Education given by a university involved in the program. The greatest hurdle to the introduction of Informatics into the educational system has been the development of qualified human resources to keep abreast of the rapid transformations inherent to this area, along with the ever-present need to improve the quality of public education. Taking part in this project, Rio Grande do Sul State, the southernmost Brazilian State, near the border with Argentina and Uruguay, created 12 NTEs across the state in which 57 multipliers (teacher trainers) were already working.

In Rio Grande do Sul, the State Commission in charge of implementing PROINFO across the state invited the Federal University of Rio Grande do Sul-UFRGS to be its partner in this endeavor. Thus, the university developed the first training program for 57 multipliers, based on a face-to-face approach. Due to the success of this course, the State asked UFRGS to stage a second course in order to train more multipliers.

Research was undertaken by the LEC (Cognitive Studies Laboratory) of UFRGS in the ongoing use of instructional technology and its role in the development of innovative educational practices. Consequently, new training methodology was developed by LEG to train the multipliers, combining face-to-face tuition with web-based Instruction to be used for distance training. This second training program started in July 1999 and ended in October 1999, involving 29 teachers from Rio do Grande do Sul State, who are expected to work as multipliers in the NTEs across the state.

TELEMATICS-BASED TRAINING

The impetus for a new training model for teacher training was based on the outcome of research developed by UFRGS in the realm of Informatics in Education. This has already been translated into theoretical models leading to new methodologies to orient changes in classroom practice, combined with the university's experience in the application of these models during the first specialization course on Informatics in Education given to the NTE multipliers of the PROINFO Program. Hence, it was concluded that it would be possible to develop and implement a second course, based on both a face-to-face approach and Internet-based distance training, the theoretical background of which was based on the development of interdisciplinary projects using Telematics.

The great challenge was to make the teachers of the public system aware of the need for incorporating new information technology in their daily practice in the classroom. The use of the technology demanded by the course facilitates the creation of learning and practice communities involving students and experts, as well as the exploration of the computer environment by both students and teachers, leading to enhanced socio-cognitive development and a shared, collective pooling of knowledge. It was expected from the positive results of the first course, that this second course would permit the elimination of learning verticality and that each teacher and student of the course, would develop his/her own learning using a shared construction model, leading to the accomplishment of autonomous knowledge.

Hence, the course was geared to stress the development of projects by small groups, addressing three aspects:

1. The student, seeking new technological resources to create knowledge leading to problem-solving related to all knowledge areas addressed in the course;
2. The teacher interacting with other teachers and with students within computerized environments in the public educational system, trying to grasp the established socio-cognitive relationships, as well as the participative, albeit autonomous knowledge-creation process; and
3. The tutor in charge of training new human resources in his/her place, attempting to understand the interdependency relationships and, at the same time, the autonomous networks created by his/her peers, as the verticality of the system is eliminated and actual cooperative and truthful relationships based on reciprocity are developed.

OPERATIONAL TRAINING TARGETS

The training under scrutiny here had the following operational targets:

1. To train the teacher trainers involved in PROINFO, through a course on Informatics in Education lasting more than 360 hours (a lato-sensu graduate course, in Brazil), to qualify them to be multipliers at the NTEs throughout Rio do Grande do Sul State;
2. To develop this 440-hour course in such a way that 320 hours of it are based on a face-to-face approach in Porto Alegre (Rio Grande do Sul State Capital), the remaining 120 hours to be dedicated to a distance training model, through the Internet; and
3. To take advantage of the 120 hours allocated to Distance Training, implementing the proposal presented in the Rio Grande do Sul State Project on Informatics in Education, in the schools assisted by each NTE, the teachers of which are attending the course.

The methodology of the course is divided into three main themes: face-to-face; mediated interaction, and distance based instruction:

1. Face-to-face-at this stage there is thematic workshops and seminars to plan and develop the interdisciplinary and diversified projects.
2. Mediated interaction-at this stage the simultaneous use of Internet services is intensified, namely: electronic mail, discussion lists, forums, real-time communication (IRG, Chat, MOOs, CuSeeMe, etc.) and, concurrently a database for storing products such as reports addressing the progress of each participant, texts, and ongoing assessment portfolios is created, all of which are generated by the students during the course. Hence, the student activity records and data collection of their production are stored. This material is published in a site located in the Internet server of the course, along with the teachers and students' home pages.
3. Distance-based instruction-at this final stage an interdisciplinary project is developed by groups of students, who are already onsite at their NTEs, by giving training to other teachers and receiving orientation through the Internet regarding their dissertation

The course is divided into the following two stages:

1. First Stage-Face-to-Face (320 hours). The first stage is compounded of two modules (Module I and 2) over eight weeks, consisting of 40 hours per week. A section known as Autonomous Production Time-APT, (eight hours per week incorporated in the 40-hour week) is programmed into this stage.

Autonomous Production Time-TPA (64 hours/activity). This time is to be used by the students in activities such as individual or collective studies, interviews with experts whose expertise is addressed in the project being developed, experiments with teachers and pupils in the classrooms, tracking of schools which are using ICT to develop pedagogical projects, finding solutions to challenges in the Informatics arena, information-searching on the Internet, data and information exchange through the Internet, instrumental software training, to name but a few.

All the communications, discussions, and reflections, as well as daily and final reports, are made available in a common area for the entire group under training, so as to permit interaction and exchange among the participants.

Module 1 (132 hours/activity). Structured into thematic workshops to be developed according to the group interests and the problems encountered by them. Each group (of three members) takes part in the thematic workshops, which are developed on a project basis approach. The first project (40 hours/activity) focuses on problem-solving to establish relationships among the different subjects of the curriculum. In this project the teachers are considered pupils addressing the basic level curriculum, formulating and solving problems, elaborating reports and evaluating their experiences.

The second project (80 hours/activity) addresses the understanding and analysis of the socio-cognitive and emotional relationships between teachers and students, and evaluates their ongoing knowledge acquisition in ICT-based learning environments. The third project lasts 12 hours on a face-to-face basis with 120 hours of distance learning. The face-to-face stage focuses on the elaboration of the teacher-training project for use of ICT in the classroom. This project is developed by each one of the NTEs involved. The second stage is developed on a distance-learning basis, focusing on implementation of the project.

Module 2 (124 hours/activity). Consists of three Basic Seminars: "New Information and Communication Technologies for Learning Environments"; "Theoretical Basis for Learning in Computerized Environments"; and "Methodologies of Educational Interaction and Intervention in Computerized Learning Environments".

2. Second Stage-Distance-Based (120 hours). This stage is held in the students' original NTEs. Each NTE (group of six students) develops an integrated project, lasting one and a half-month, being both theoretical and practical, based on their experiences with the students on the course and on their experience with the students of the schools

belonging to each NTE. Geared towards motivating·the students of the Basic Level to build relevant knowledge in computerized environments, the teachers involved in this experience are supported in the cooperative construction of relevant knowledge to assist the students in the computerized environment. They are also assisted in the construction of sharing methodology for interaction and intervention. They are encouraged to use the available ICT as enablers in this process. In this stage, the mentors of the course assist the students of the course on a distance-basis approach, through the Internet.

Assessment generally has at least one of the following three purposes: (a) to improve, (b) to inform, and/or (c) to verify. The aims of this assessment are to provide information that can be used to determine whether or not intended outcomes are being achieved and how the project can be improved. In addition, the assessment process was structured to inform decision-makers about relevant issues that affect the project. In this assessment process, it is important to distinguish between "formative" and "summative" assessment. Formative assessment is the collection of data and feedback of results on an ongoing basis. Formative assessment is designed to provide information for the purpose of improving the project or process being assessed. Summative assessment is designed to produce information that can be used to make decisions about the overall success of the project or process. Hence, this is a summative assessment.

To conduct this research some actions were undertaken and a theoretical framework was used. Several steps were conducted, to develop a working methodology to be applied in this research task. These steps are listed as follows:

- The project is presented in detail as conceived by its creators;
- The modus-operandi of the Program, that is, its structure, is presented to make clear how the outcomes are intended to be accomplished;
- Data is collected to be analyzed. In this case the following data was collected:

- The rationale of the project taken from academic papers developed to depict the program itself;
- student portfolios and projects deployed on the Internet also made available-although in a reserved area-through permission granted by the training coordinators;
- Analysis of the outcome of the project obtained from the application and consolidation of questionnaires and interviews with both the students and teachers involved; and
- Classroom observations and video-recordings, to analyze whether the teachers trained in a constructivist environment are applying this approach to train their students-the other teachers of the public education system;

- Comparison between the forecast and actual accomplished objectives so as to evaluate the program;
- Analysis of the cost-effectiveness of the Program;
- Conclusions and analysis of the strengths and weaknesses of the training program.

THEORETICAL FRAMEWORK

The questionnaire and direct observation of the training, mainly the web-based instruction (WBI) stage were heavily drawn from the paper: "Effective Dimensions of Interactive Learning on the World Wide Web," Reeves and Reeves (1997). This model has applications in research, implementation and evaluation of web-based instruction programs such as this project.

The proposed model includes ten dimensions of interactive learning on the World Wide Web (WWW or Web): (a) pedagogical philosophy, (b) learning theory, (c) goal orientation, (d) task orientation, (e) source of motivation, (f) teacher role, (g) metacognitive support, (h) collaborative learning, (i) cultural sensitivity, and (j) structural flexibility. Each of the 10 dimensions in this model is presented as a two-ended continuum with contrasting values at either end.

Needless to say, the world is rarely dichotomous and there is more complexity involved in learning than any of these dimensions represent. However, the individual dimensions themselves are not as important as the interplay among the 10 dimensions that represent the instructional designs of various WBI sites.

1. Pedagogical philosophy (Instructivist <=> Constructivist). The debate between instructivist and constructivist approaches to teaching and learning continues through education and training. Instructivists stress the importance of objectives that exit apart from the learner. Little emphasis is placed on learners per se, who are viewed as passive recipients of instructions or treated as empty vessels to be filled with learning. By contrast, constructivists emphasize the primacy of the learner's intentions, experience, and cognitive strategies. According to constructivists, learners construct different cognitive structures based upon their previous knowledge and what they experience in different learning environments. It is paramount for constructivists that learning environments be as rich and diverse as possible. Instead of an empty vessel, the learner is regarded as an individual replete with preexisting motivations, experiences, aptitudes, and knowledge. Tasks to be accomplished and problems to be solved must have personal relevance to the learner. The constructivists believe that what we know is constructed-both individually and socially-based on prior experience.
2. Learning theory (Behavioural <=> Cognitive). According to behaviourists, the critical factor in learning is observable behaviour, and instruction involves shaping desirable behaviours through the arrangement of stimuli, responses, feedback, and reinforcement. A stimulus is provided (e.g., a short presentation of content), then a response is elicited, often by way of a question. Feedback is given as to the accuracy of the response, and positive reinforcement is given for accurate responses. Inaccurate responses result in a repetition of the original stimulus, and the cycle

begins again. Cognitive psychologists place more emphasis on internal mental states than on behaviour. A cognitive taxonomy of internal learning states includes simple propositions, schema, rules, skills, mental models, and so forth. They claim that a variety of strategies-including memorization, direct instruction, deduction, drill and practice, and induction, are required in any learning environment, depending upon the type of knowledge to be created by the learner.

3. Goal orientation (Sharp <=> Broad). The goals for education and training can range from sharply focused ones to general higher-order ones. Hence, the goal orientation of WBI systems varies in degree of focus from sharp to broad.
4. Task orientation (Academic <=> Authentic). The context of learning is enormously important to adults. An academic design would depend heavily on having the learners' carry out traditional academic exercises. By contrast, an authentic design would engage the adults in practical activities such as preparing job applications, thereby situating practice and feedback within realistic scenarios. If knowledge, skills, and attitudes are learned in a practical context, they will be used in that and similar contexts.
5. Source of motivation (Extrinsic <=> Intrinsic). Motivation is a primary factor in any theory or model of learning. Every new educational technology promises to be intrinsically motivating. This dimension ranges from extrinsic (i.e., outside the learning environment) to intrinsic (i.e., integral to the learning environment). Intrinsically, motivation instruction is elusive regardless of the delivery systems.
6. Teacher role (Didactic <=> Facilitative). The teacher role continuum ranges from didactic to facilitative. In the former role, the teacher presents information and asks learners to memorize information and recall it later in tests. The latter role assigns cognitive responsibility to the learners, as they should be responsible for recognizing

and judging patterns of information, organizing data, constructing alternative perspectives, and presenting new knowledge in meaningful ways, wherein the teachers are mentors and tutors of this process.

7. Metacognitive support (Unsupported <=> Integrated). Metacognition refers to a learner's awareness of objectives, ability to plan and evaluate learning strategies, and capacity to monitor progress and adjust learning behaviour to accommodate needs. The metacognitive support dimension is unsupported at one end of the continuum and integrated at the other. Recapitulation of the students' strategies at any point in the problem-solving process, as well as construction of web-based portfolios are examples of how support for reflection and metacognition might be provided in WBI.
8. Collaborative learning strategies. The Collaborative Learning dimension ranges from a complete lack of support for collaboration to the inclusion of collaborative learning as an integral feature. Cooperative and collaborative learning refers to instructional methods in which learners work together in pairs or small groups to accomplish shared goals.
9. Cultural sensitivity. All instructional systems have cultural implications. In an insensitive approach the training is developed regardless of the culture and diversity of the learners it is intended to address. On the other hand, a respectful approach should be based on the diversity in the populations where the system will be used so that the overall learning environment is enhanced. It is unlikely that WBI Training can be designed to adapt to every cultural norm, but sites should be designed to be as culturally sensitive as possible.
10. Structural flexibility. "Fixed" systems, still dominant in education, are usually limited to specific places, for example, a classroom or laboratory, at specific times or 50 minutes class periods. Independent of time and/or location constraints, the learner can use "Open" systems. The Web provides opportunities for more asynchronous

(open) learning, although some web-based learning tools are temporally fixed (synchronous), such as chats, video-conferences, MOOs, and MUDs.

THEORETICAL MODEL OF TRAINING APPLIED BY THE LEC

The Cognitive Studies Laboratory (LEC) has published several papers addressing a socio- constructivist approach to train teachers using Information and Communication Technologies as enablers. According to LEC the answer to the question: "If new practices are recommended to the teachers under training, why do the trainers themselves not apply this approach in their own classes?" lies in the lack of a theoretical frame of reference upon which this practice is based.

To design a new pedagogical model for computerized environments, it is necessary to create a theoretical framework which leads the teachers to understand more fully the affective and socio-cognitive processes that are developed when students are interacting with information and communication technologies. This theoretical approach is even more necessary considering that the digital media increases the interactive processes among the players involved (teachers, students, experts, community). This model can assist in developing interactive models for teacher training.

TECHNOLOGICAL RATIONALITY

As already stated, the design of the course is based on two different but complementary moments: (a) face-to-face and (b) distance-basis, having as its rationale an interactive and problem-solving methodology and leading to a central axis relying on the development of interdisciplinary projects using telematic tools as enablers. As can be seen, the training is heavily constructivist-based and student-centered, aiming to develop interdisciplinary skills in the trainees (multipliers), so that they can use this expertise in their classrooms to train other teachers. Hence, the main target of this chapter is to know whether the training-albeit developed according to this constructivist paradigm-was successful in developing a new classroom practice, which was observed when the trainees were back to their NTEs to continue the training of their peers.

WEB-BASED STRUCTURE OF THE TRAINING

The LEC of the Federal University of Rio Grande do Sul did not use any kind of off-the-shelf software package to develop the course. As real constructivists, they preferred not be restricted to a hermetic, Instructionist, and behaviouristic system, but to build their own web-environment during the training. Since the beginning of the training, technology-mediated activities were developed by way of Internet services such as e-mail, discussion lists, newsgroups, real time communication (IRC, MOOs, CuSeeMe, etc.), and spaces to store the practical and theoretical records of the groups, as well as contributions from the group.

The site has a public area and a protected zone reserved only for the participants of the course. In the public space, all the navigators have the following resources at their disposal:

- Support and Interactive resources, such as information about the course, a library offering articles and research papers, links to interesting sites, IRC, FAQs, a Guest Book, and News about the Project;
- Learning projects of the groups of multipliers that offer partial considerations resulting from the analytical work addressing the developed processes and data obtained to date; and
- Individual portfolios that encompass student home pages, student diaries (relating their reflections about the student-teacher processes developed both in individual and collective moments); their theoretical output and a space to store collaborative and cooperative contributions.

In the reserved area, one can find:

- Group portfolios that keep texts and articles generated by discussions developed in a collective way, texts under production by the group, enabled by the theoretical skill that has been developed through the discussions undertaken in the listserv of the site;

- Orientation for the dissertations to be developed by the NTE's groups. In this space, methodological suggestions of the tutors, reports about the implementation of the NTEs in each region and records of the exchanges between tutors and students are made available; and
- The Cyber Cafe-a meeting point to foment informal exchanges, jokes, invitations, and so forth.

On the course site, the students can upload their information through forms previously developed as templates. This information is immediately converted to HTML code and stored on the site. In this manner, their reflections, experiences, reports, critics, data to be used in shared projects, and so forth can be easily deployed in the Web.

LEC'S COURSE EVALUATION

The qualitative evaluation of the course, according to LEC's approach, was based on the following elements addressing the students:

- Regular construction and publishing of the individual and collective production on the course website;
- Creation and publication of multimedia documents;
- Contribution in the shared spaces on the site;
- Publishing, follow-up and discussion of the projects developed; and
- Personal use of the website resources, both in a synchronous and asynchronous way.

A system (AccessWatch) was used to record interaction among the students and between students and teachers. Subsequently, the quality of the interaction was analyzed. All evaluation was based on the process of knowledge creation, established by analysis of student portfolios, project evolution, student reflections, and student self-analysis developed throughout the course. We can conclude that according to LEC's evaluation factors, the training program was a success. The trained teachers are aware of the need to change their pedagogical practices, and they now know how to do that and are willing to deploy what they have learned in their schools, as soon as possible.

THEORY VERSUS PRACTICE

The practical training given by the multipliers (trained teachers) to the other teachers in a cascade process complies with the way they were trained, that is, they try to apply the socio-constructivist approach in the training, using Information Technology as a tool and enabler to give a new awareness to the teachers about how to spur the students to create their own knowledge. At one point one of the multipliers-almost as a throwback to her old mental model-tried to help a student by giving her the correct way of solving a problem. This should be considered normal, as the multipliers themselves are still undergoing their own transformation process, which takes time.

Care and empathy are used all the time, just in the same way as they were used in the multipliers' training. They understand the deconstruction process the students are experiencing as they have been through the same process themselves. Coherence is the key-word for the success of the training, and the students see this as the multipliers' discourse and practice leading the course to the same central objectives, namely to use the technology to create a new modus-operandi in the classroom, thereby enabling the students to create and socialize their knowledge.

Naturally, coherence is not the only issue in the transformation of pedagogical practice, but it is paramount for the success of the training itself. The use of the framework developed by Pettigrew and Whipp (1991) can help us to better understand the role of coherence in the success of the training and, by extension, of teacher practice. This model can show one of the possible ways to achieve a successful strategic change in the educational realm.

BARRIERS TO BE OVERCOME

The greatest mistake one can make is to conclude that

training itself is enough to change pedagogical practice in schools. Developed by Pascale and Athos (1982) and Peters and Water-man (1982) and adapted by the researcher for the educational realm, several issues in the educational environment are interrelated, thus a deep and actual change affect all of them.

The seven S's are defined as:

- Strategy-the route the school has chosen to be successful;
- Structure-the organizational structure of the school;
- Systems-the procedures and processes that make the school work;
- Style-the way the school conducts its mission, epitomized especially by those at the top;
- Staff-the pool of teachers who need to be developed, challenged and encouraged;
- Skills-not just the collection of the skills the school has but the particular combinations it has to excel; and
- Superordinate Goals-this means goals "of a higher order" and expresses the values, concepts and visions the teachers and principals bring to the school.

Analyzing the use of ICT in the schools after teacher training in a WBI constructivist environment, we can conclude that:

- Strategy-if the school principal is trained in the use of ICT to develop a new pedagogical practice, it will become easier for the school to adopt a new praxis. However, it is important to say that the schools' strategy must conform to the educational strategy developed by the state government as a whole.
- Structure-this is perhaps the most difficult issue to be changed as the public authorities, themselves, have designed the school's organizational structure. As Chandler (1962) said: "Structure follows Strategy," so they are intimately linked. Hence, a radical change in the organizational design of the schools is essential in order to reach a new level of pedagogical practice, which is more open, constructivist and child-centered, otherwise newly developed strategies will fail.

- Systems-ICT can dramatically change the pedagogical procedures and processes applied by the schools, by reengineering and innovating old and outdated processes.
- Style-as the style depends heavily on each school principal's way of guiding them, it is important to have the headmasters trained in how to use ICT in a constructivist way.
- Staff-teachers trained in ICT can socialize the benefits of the new educational approach by explaining and demonstrating the use of ICT to their peers in the school, thus becoming catalysts in the transformation process.
- Skills-once again, this is an issue the training can deal with successfully.
- Superordinate Goals-the training gives the teachers new values, concepts, and visions about education and the role ICT can play in the classroom. By consequence, it can lead to a (r)evolution in school practice, so as to break with the old schemata (mental models) and define a new vision and mission for the school.

Now, we may depict the framework already presented, highlighting the "dark" nodes of the model as the ones which a socio-constructivist approach associated to the use of ICT are unable to change or influence in a deeper way. So, by consequence, these items need to be addressed through the use of other strategies rather than via teacher training.

THE INFLUENCE OF CARE IN THE TRAINING PROCESS

We can thus see that care is fundamental in knowledge creation, as explained by von Krogh (1998). According to Maturana and Varela (1987), cognition is a creative act of conjuring up a microcosm. Because knowledge resides in our bodies and is closely tied to our senses and previous experience, we will naturally create a world in ways which are unique to ourselves. In this study, care engenders trust in the learning process and also gives rise to active empathy, making it possible to assess and understand what the other person needs. Empathy is the attempt to put yourself in another's shoes, understanding his/her particular situation, interests, skill level, history of success and failures, and future opportunities and problems.

By means of active empathy, you proactively seek to understand the other person. Through active questioning and acute observation, you seek out instances where your efforts are needed. You practice dialogue rather than advocating only your own point of view. Care accomplishes precisely the sharing of positive and negative emotions through active empathy. In this study, for example, the relationship between the student and the teacher in learning the use of Informatics in the classroom is made easier when the teacher explains that he/she has had some of the same personal frustrations in learning a specific issue, and that speed in grasping the d ifficulty of this issue is not a gauge of the intellectual capacity of the student, but one of the inherent characteristics of a long learning process.

Hence, it can be concluded that the approach developed in this specific training for knowledge creation was based on von Krogh. As there is care in training, there is mutual trust, active empathy, access to help among team members, lenient judgments towards participants in the team, and courage. In such a situation the student will bestow knowledge on others as well as receive active help from others (others bestowing knowledge on him/her). The environment is supportive, and the goal of the learning process shifts from obtaining "maximum grip" to reaching "maximum leverage" on others' knowledge. There is a mutual intent to help others to optimize their task performance, and therefore, to share knowledge. The individual can experiment more freely to develop unconventional task solutions, and is emboldened in the pursuit of knowledge creation.

The individual is integrated into the team. Other students and teachers take an active interest in the learning process, and the individual is encouraged to make knowledge explicit while learning. When care runs high, colleagues show interest and support, and the individual member can spontaneously articulate his/her knowledge using unconventional language, metaphors, and analogies. Expressing personal difficulties in knowledge creation will be met with leniencey from other team members and active feedback will be provided.

The process of mutual bestowing provides fertile ground for a distinct process of creating social knowledge in a team: Indwelling. Indwelling is of particular importance to the sharing of tacit knowledge and concept creation. Polanyi and Prosch (1975) suggested that dwelling in a concept can be understood as a dramatic shift of perspectives, changing the concept from "looking at" to "looking with." In broader terms, indwelling is about commitment to an idea, to an experience, to a concept, or to a fellow human being. In developing shared tacit knowledge, the challenge for the teachers in knowledge creation is to dwell in the experiences, perspectives, and concepts of other participants, or in other words, to change from self-commitment to commitment to others.

In changing such deeper-level commitments, participants literally make changes in their perceptions. When care runs high, team members extend help to each other in finding new means of conveying and sharing personal beliefs. Trust and lenience make it easier to articulate emotional aspects of an experience, as was realized during this research. Again, it is important to stress that the emotional component, here translated as care, was a vital force for the success of this socio-constructivist WBI training.

Socio-constructivist training demands by its very nature high involvement of the teachers, both in the face-to-face and the distance-based stages. As the training aims to lead the students to reprogramming their minds by challenging their "temporary certainties," some physical as well as emotional support is necessary. The students are conveyed to an "unlearn" and "re-learn" process, and sometimes they offload their mental models without having acquired new schemata. At this moment care is absolutely necessary as they are emotionally deconstructed.

COSTS

The socio-constructivist paradigm leads naturally to higher costs than those involved in traditional methods. The teachers must be very much involved with the students, as both the success of training and the accomplishment of objectives depend on the knowledge socialization process and on care as previously mentioned. All of this leads to a higher number of man-hours, resulting in a higher total cost per capita than that expected in traditional web-based instruction training.

It can be concluded that instructionist and behaviouristic WBI training lead to lower costs than those involved in traditional face-to-face training. However, as this training relies on a constructivist approach, the savings through the use of Internet in the distance-based instruction is counterbalanced by the great involvement among the players during the face-to-face stage. Training such as this could hardly accomplish its main targets without face-to-face moments. Care cannot be developed to maximum potential with a purely distance-based approach. The main challenge faced was to research the ideal percentage of face-to-face and distance-based moments required in constructivist training as a whole.

TRADITIONAL VERSUS SOCIO-CONSTRUCTIVIST WEB-BASED TRAINING

As final recommendations that can improve the training analyzed above, we should highlight the following issues to be implemented:

1. Mentoring programs. Mentoring programs must motivate the trained teachers to share their knowledge with junior teachers and newcomers in the schools. Management can achieve this by defining two sets of responsibilities for each individual, namely to develop proportionally his! her ability to acquire expertise, in line with the responsibility to make his/her help accessible to those who need it as his/her expertise grows.
2. Headmaster training. As previously stated, the role of the headmaster in the creation of a "new school" is paramount,

not just to motivate the teachers, but also to be fully involved in the other realms that hinder a true, radical transformation in the pedagogical practice. Hence, their participation and involvement in the training process is highly important for training targets to be fully accomplished.

3. Social events. It is important to reunite the trained teachers in social events, where in a face-to-face basis they can share the experiences, improvements and obstacles they are facing. These moments are as important as opening and maintaining a newsgroup on the Internet the participants of which are already trained in this socio-constructivist approach.

FUTURE RESEARCH

Future research is recommended addressing two central issues:

- The ideal percentage of face-to-face and Internet distance-based approach in socio-constructivist teacher training such as the case analyzed; and
- The gender influence in training outcomes, as we saw clearly that care is paramount for the success of the endeavor and that care impacts differently upon men and women while under training.

All in all, this was a very innovative teacher training initiative which fully complied with the trainers' paradigms and pedagogical philosophies, seeking coherence at all times. Undoubtedly, as stated before, this alone will not change the outdated former teaching and learning praxis, but it is an updated and powerful enabler for instilling the necessary changes in the other remaining areas addressed in the whole educational process.

5

Gender Towards Technology

After five years of teaching interactive technology and game design at a large Midwestern university, one of us noticed an apparent positive correlation between students who spent a lot of time playing complex digital games and a willingness to engage actively with technically complicated interactive media design. Students, who spent a lot of time playing with and on their computers exhibited a higher level of comfort with technology, often personally assembled and repaired their own computers, and cheerfully took on challenging tasks and assignments. There were always significantly fewer females than males in this category of students. This study sought to explore if exposure to digital play might increase female involvement in technologically complex activity.

One of the premises behind the enactment of Title IX legislation in the United States is that equality of opportunity in sports and play relates to equality of opportunity in the society at large. Although it was a subject of contentious debate for years, it is now largely accepted that the presence and level of performance of women in sports reflects equality of opportunity and parity in work and other non-play sectors. Play is an important means through which societal norms are taught and reified. Females are making great strides in achieving equality of participation in a wide range of r activities.

Michelle Wie, for example is proving not only that women can excel, but that they can do so on the same playing field as men. This chapter considers the notion that engaging in complex technologically mediated play is an important factor in the development of a pro-technology outlook and that gender equality in participation in digital play is as important as it is in traditional analog play.

COMPUTER GAMEPLAY

Although much has been accomplished in leveling the playing field for females in whole-body play environments, computerized gameplay has long been male-oriented and male-dominated. There are many types of play available in digital media. Some of these are digital replicas of analog games such as gin, euchre, chess, or solitaire. In general, these games do not present the player with challenges beyond those of the scope of the analog game. Other types of games exist only through the digital matrix of the computer. In the more complex games of this type, the game world itself is a digital construction and the player must learn and understand not only the culture of the game (such as languages, behaviours, and physical coordination skills), but also the technical interface that makes the game possible.

Most of the latter type of digital games are designed and produced by males for largely male audiences. Lucas and Sherry (2004) define traditional games (those preferred by females) as "non-mental rotation games" and the latter (preferred by males) as "mental rotation games." These terms suggest that playing "mental rotation" games requires an additional level of training and immersion not required by traditional games. We utilize Lucas and Sherry's terms for these games throughout the paper. Additionally, gender biases in the analog world are often perpetuated and reinforced in digital environments. This was demonstrated very concretely in economist Castronova's study of the monetary value of avatars. Despite the fact that male and female avatars have exactly the same skills and capacities, he found that players paid more for male avatars than for female ones when purchasing them in online auctions.

Although females are now as likely as males to play on computers, females are much more likely to play digital replicas of analog games. The majority of players of complex, intellectually and physically challenging, extremely immersive games, such as HALO, Medal of Honor, Madden Football, Tony Hawk, and Grand Theft Auto, are males. There is, however, a committed and engaged minority of females who play traditionally male games. Versterby's (2005) dissertation on female Counter-Strike players in Denmark documents this phenomenon while underlining how unusual they are. MMPORPGs like World of Warcraft have a significant and growing population of female gamers. Clearly women can play these games, and play them as competitively as males. This study seeks to determine if there is a positive correlation between such gameplay and feelings of competence in relation to technology.

GENDERED PLAY/RELATIONSHIP TO TECHNOLOGY

Much has been written about the negative effects of the lack of female participation in digital gaming. These include stereotypical representation of females in computer games resulting in digital environments in which females feel uncomfortable, perpetuation of the ethos that computers and technology are the realm of males to the exclusion of females, and the disinclination of females to engage in either digital play or technologically demanding professions. In addition, the disinclination of women to enroll in computer science classes and to pursue degrees in computer-related disciplines has been a topic of concern for universities, governments, and scholars for some time. Southern Methodist University, for example, has instituted a "Game Development Scholarship for Women" in an attempt to attract more women to the field.

The British government is establishing financial incentives to attract women to science and technology careers (Public Technology.Net, 2004). According to Margolis and Fisher's study (2002) on why women drop out of computer science programs, the social/cultural perceptions of technology as a male domain are a significant factor in dissuading women. Similarly Barnett and Rivers (2004) make a compelling case that the barriers to women engaging in these fields are cultural constructions.

Most recently, in response to Lawrence Summers' conjecture that perhaps women are intrinsically worse at science than men, the American Academy of Sciences published a report entitled "Beyond Bias and Barriers: Fulfilling the Potential of Women in Academic Science and Engineering" This report contends that attitudes towards women in science and technology careers have a much more significant impact on performance than biological factors. Social and cultural gender norms are established and reified through play; thus, they can be influenced through play as well.

DEFINITIONS OF PLAY

One of the difficulties in doing research in the areas of "play" and "fun" is coming to an understanding of what these terms mean. Philosophers have understood play as a way for humans to create meaningful worlds that are separate and different from the world in which we find ourselves. Huizinga defines play as "voluntary activity ... freedom ... not 'ordinary' or 'real' life ... In the form and function of play, itself an independent entity which is senseless and irrational, man's consciousness that he is embedded in a sacred order of things finds its first, highest and holiest expression".

Gadamer has a chapter entitled "Play as the Clue to Ontological Explanation" in which he states that "Play fulfills its purpose only if the player loses himself in play". And Csikszentmihalyi and Bennett state that "Play is action generating action: a unified experience flowing from one moment to the next in contradiction to our otherwise disjoint 'everyday' experiences". Play for philosophers is thus an internal state more than an externally existing event. Whether or not an activity is play is based on the experience of the player, not the activity itself. This makes play rather difficult to operationalize and measure.

Play has been studied in animals, where its importance is very clear even if exactly how it is important has eluded researchers. Tayler and Saayman (1973) noted that:

It is generally agreed that the predisposition to manipulate, explore and exhibit advanced object-play is a fundamental prerequisite for the emergence of the skillful use of tools (Jay, 1968) for which the primate, both anatomically and neurologically, has been admirably selected by evolutionary pressure.

Grandin & Johnson (2005) discuss the lack of research on play in general and summarize the research on reasons for and causes of animal play in their recent book. They review current research on animal play and conclude that:

When you look at what animals do when they're playing, and put that together with the fact that animals do the most physical play while the cerebellum is forming connections, I think we'll probably find out that play is an important way that a young animal develops its brain to guide active movement.

For humans, play is as important for tool acquisition and locomotor function development as it is in animals. Ellis (1973) believes that play was and is essential to human evolution and the ability to adapt to new environments:

Thus stimulus events and configurations in the environment that are novel, complex, and dissonant elevate arousal and to the extent this moves an individual toward an optimal level, it is accompanied by positive affect or pleasure. The kinds of behaviours engendered by such reinforcement are exploration, investigation and manipulation. This process leads to increased knowledge of the conditions and consequences of the environment over and above the immediate satisfaction of basic survival needs. Play fosters the behavioural variability of an individual, and therefore a species, and thereby increases the probability of future adaptation to unpredictable circumstances.

Another way to approach an understanding of play is through the concept of 'fun.' In our cultural understanding, play is something that we do because it is fun; it is enjoyable, pleasurable, the opposite of duty, tedium, and obligation. Malone, one of the earliest researchers to discuss fun in an academic context, defines it as "intrinsically motivating"; that is to say, behaviour that is enjoyable for its own sake and not for any perceived utility. He, too, like the philosophers of play, defines play by what it is not, and emphasizes the distinction between fun and utility just as philosophical definitions of play emphasize the distinction between play and "real" life.

Given the wide range of meanings and associations for the words "fun" and "play," we decided to avoid attempting to define them. In our study we simply asked respondents to tell us about the activities that they consider as play and activities that they do for fun. We conflate the concepts of play and fun; a play activity is something that is done for fun or because it is fun, however the respondents chose to interpret these terms.

IMPORTANCE OF PLAY AND FUN

Willingness and ability to play in digital environments matter because play is political; that is to say that play is related to the practice and exercise of power and pleasure within given environments. This study seeks to determine some of the effects of playing-the experience of pleasure mediated through a computer-on players' relationship to the technology that mediates it. It makes sense intuitively that people want to spend time in environments that are pleasurable for them, but remarkably little research has been conducted on the topic of "fun."

In 1988, Carroll and Thomas argued that fun is a very important part of human computer interaction and that "fun is potentially very important in its own right. From this, we reason that there is an important need to develop a research program in fun and motivation". Lack of existing research is due partly to the fact that researchers are concerned that fun won't be taken seriously as an object of study. Some researchers have done studies utilizing the word "fun" while others have changed the word to "enjoyment." Webster and Martocchio (1992) used the word "playfulness." Csikszentmihalyi (1991) integrated fun into his concept of "flow."

Yi and Hwang's (2003) work examines technology acceptance and willingness to engage with computer-based tools in relation to enjoyment. They conducted a study to determine if self-reported enjoyment and measurement of self-efficacy had an effect on subjects' willingness to utilize a web-based instructional system. They found that as enjoyment increased, so did use; even if the technology itself was difficult to use. Agarwal and Krarhanna (2000) argue that "fun" is an important consideration when examining user relationships to technology and that fun factors significantly in technology use and immersion. A recent pilot study on pleasure and new media determined that "Central to the findings is that while pleasure and displeasure are largely undertheorized, these terms, when deployed empirically, afford a useful entry point into evaluating media experiences."

Bandura's self-efficacy theory states that a person's relationship to him/herself and to a task makes a difference in terms of how well a person will perform that task. If participants feel as though they are going to do a task well, if they feel powerful in relation to that task, then they are likely to perform that task well. If they have low expectations of their ability to perform, then they tend to perform poorly. Bandura has published extensively on the relationship between self-efficacy and the ability to perform tasks, as well as producing scales that can be modified to assess self-efficacy under a variety of different circumstances. Csikszentmihalyi (1991) and Csikszentmihalyi and Bennett (1971) describe performance during a state of "flow" or in-depth immersion which is often experienced during play activities or activities that are considered "fun."

RELATIONSHIP BETWEEN PLAY AND SELF-EFFICACY

The current study hypothesizes that there is a relationship between the amount of time subjects spend deriving enjoyment or experiencing fun while engaging in digitally mediated activities and self-efficacy in relation to computer technologies. We extend Ellis's (1973) postulation that humans use play as a means of seeking arousal and becoming proficient in new environments to digitally mediated environments. We can relate the amount of time users spend playing a game to how compelling and relevant the game environment is for the player. Studies on play have determined that one of the essential features of a good game is that the level of challenge or difficulty of the game must be matched to the player's ability. In order to enjoy a game, the player has to feel as though he/she might be able to win it, though the victory cannot be too easily obtained.

One of the reasons that digital play is so compelling is that the level of difficulty can be adjusted to the level of the player's ability much more precisely than is possible in most analog games. In Bandura's terms, we can say that experienced digital game players are very good at maintaining a high level of self-efficacy in relation to the technology that makes the gameplay possible. This study also seeks to determine relationships between gender, amount of time devoted to play (both analog and computer-based play), and attitudes towards technology.

Some researchers attempt to measure fun and play-related concepts such as "enjoyment" in terms of technology. Investigating the correlation between the concepts of "enjoyment" and usefulness, they operationalize fun in order to measure the acceptance of and engagement with specific software or hardware technologies. These researchers successfully utilize adaptations of Bandura's (2001) self-efficacy scales in their work. Our scales are based on theirs.

FEMALE ENGAGEMENT WITH DIGITAL PLAY AND TECHNOLOGY

Historically, women play differently and less than men in an array of different cultures. Play is practice with power and when women lack power within a culture, they are also refused permission to play. The first lines of professional basketball player Mariah Burton Nelson's 1994 book on women in sports demonstrate that social norms are enforced through what are considered acceptable and not acceptable play behaviours:

> If you grew up female in America, you heard this: Sports are unfeminine. And this: Girls who play sports are tomboys or lesbians. You got this message: Real women don't spend their free time sliding feet-first into home plate or smacking their fists into soft leather gloves.

A walk through the aisles at Toys "R" Us makes clear that practically from birth, play tools-toys-remain rigidly gendered. Studies confirm that children are aware of gender from a very young age and make choices in play based on gender appropriateness. It is unsurprising therefore that gender differences persist in digital play environments. Traditional gendered play norms, however, are being challenged in many sports. Females now compete with and against males in football, wrestling, and golf, among others. Females who challenge traditional gender norms garner a great deal of media attention. When Anika Sorenstam dared to challenge the men of the PGA, for example, a media blitz ensued.

One of the purposes of this exploratory study is to see if play norms are changing in a conservative state in Middle America. We do not claim findings which are generalizable to different populations in other parts of the country. The most recent Pew report states that female rates of engagement in online computer play equal those of males. Although much of this gameplay is of the non-mental rotation type mentioned earlier, such data suggests that female attitudes towards computer-based play are changing and that there might also be gains in female attitudes towards technological aptitude and computer self-efficacy. This study seeks to determine if women who engage in technological play report higher self-efficacy towards technology than those who do not.

Taylor (2003) examined why some women enjoy the complex gameplay of online virtual communities. She suggests that women's participation in online game worlds can best be understood by analyzing the kinds of pleasure that women derive from engaging in these worlds:

Rather than seeing this group of players [women] as an anomaly, this chapter explores how focusing on the pleasures women derive from gaming might lead to more complex understanding of both gender and computer games.

During a pretest for this study, some female respondents stated that it was difficult for them to give themselves permission to play. They felt that there were so many pressures on their lives, so many things to get done in a day, for example, that play was not an acceptable use of their time unless it was somehow useful to them. Some stated, for example, that they engaged in something like running both because it was fun and because it kept them fit. We did not encounter a similar response among male respondents and thus decided to test to see if whether or not an activity was considered useful made a difference in terms of time spent engaging in that activity and how fun respondents rated it.

RESEARCH HYPOTHESES

This study examines adult play behaviours in digital and non-digital environments. The expectation, based on market data and cultural norms, is that males spend more time playing than females do. Part of the scope of the study is to allow respondents to self-define what play is for them. Thus it is expected that females will report behaviours not traditionally considered play (home decorating, chatting, shopping, etc.) as play.

Given that play is gendered from birth, we expect to see gender differences in the types of games played. Given that the audience for "mental rotation games" is largely male, it is expected that males will spend more money on this kind of digital play (which generally involves more expensive software and hardware). We hypothesize that those who experience more pleasure from digital environments will score higher on scales measuring levels of self-efficacy related to computer environments.

H1. There will be gender differences in types of activities recorded as play. Males will spend more time playing overall and spend more time engaged in digital play.

Given that so many digital games are designed to appeal to male appetites (war, shooting and action games; games where females are represented primarily as sexual objects for the male gaze) and that more males play complex digital games involving consoles and software, it is expected that males will report spending more money on equipment for digital play.

H2. Males will spend more money on software and hardware for digital play.

Anecdotal data suggest that women find it more difficult to give themselves permission to play and to engage in activities only for fun. We would expect that males are more willing to engage in activities only because they are fun. To further explore this issue, questions were asked about whether or not respondents felt guilty about devoting time to play.

H3. It is expected that females will be more likely to report play that is useful, will be less likely to enjoy "mental rotation" play, and will report more guilt in association with play.

Digital play is a form of pleasure-seeking behaviour. Since most pleasure-producing digital environments are designed by males for a historically male audience, it is expected that males will report experiencing more fun while engaged in these activities. If females do participate in these activities, it is expected that their reasons for doing so will be different from the reasons given by males. If females are not engaging in them for fun, they might provide other reasons for doing so. Given that current data suggest that women are playing online games in increasing numbers, we expect differences in the type of digital play reported based on types of digital game.

Given the importance of fun/enjoyment as a factor in technology acceptance, it is expected that those who report more pleasure in association with computer-based environments will also interact with computers more easily and report a greater sense of self-efficacy than those who do not associate computers with pleasure.

H4. Those who report using digital environments for play, will rate higher on measures of self-efficacy/technophilia than those who don't. Males are more likely to experience digitally mediated play and will rate higher on the technophilia index.

Both sexes devote large amounts of time to play activities and both see this category of behaviour as being an important part of their lives. They largely agree with the statement "Play makes my life richer and more enjoyable." The average hours per week spent engaging in play activities is 34.8 (SD = 42.3). Given the reluctance of some respondents to fill out the questionnaire at all, it is possible that people actually play more than they think they do. More research is required to further explore these questions.

Males currently spend more money on hardware and software for digital play than females do. In economic terms, men seem more willing to accept a financial cost for digital pleasure than women, despite the fact that females report enjoying digital play as much as males do. We expected that females would report enjoying console play less than males (due to the frequent stereotypical representations of females in console play) but this hypothesis was not supported. Future studies should continue to investigate female economic investment in technology given the increasing numbers of females playing MMPORGs like World of Warcraft, which require a monthly subscription fee but not a heavy investment in console technology.

The results that we obtained in terms of gender attitudes towards usefulness, fun, and guilt demonstrate that there is a great deal more research to be done in this area. There were several gender differences in the types of behaviours recorded as being fun. Females are more likely to report communication-based behaviours such as IM and on-line worlds as fun and are more likely to cite communication as a reason why a play activity is useful. Females report shopping as a play activity more than males do and are much less likely to engage in body-intensive and complex console-driven computer play. When we remove shopping and home decorating from the body-intensive play grouping, females are less likely to say that they engage in these activities because they are fun and significantly more likely to say that they do so because it is useful (fitness, lose weight).

These findings suggest that females are, as expected, less likely to engage in activities traditionally defined as play. Historically and philosophically, play has been valued as a way of developing and strengthening the body and the mind. Body-intensive play activities develop respect for the physical self and an understanding of how to extend the body's abilities through challenge and practice. Complex computer games combine physical and mental challenges in digital environments. Many console games require a great deal of specialized physical dexterity in order to manipulate the interface properly. These games often include many layers of intellectual complexity, which allow players to play at a level that challenges them.

These findings confirm that participation in these activities is still primarily male. The results of this study suggest that there may be a correlation between "mental rotation" play and technophilia. Females who do engage in such play are just as likely to enjoy it and to derive benefits from it. Counter to expectations, women do not report feeling more guilty about the amount of time they spend playing than men do. Given that men are more likely to agree with the statement "Others would prefer that I play less," it appears that they are more likely to be criticized than women for spending time playing. This may simply be due to the fact that men spend more time playing, but it may also mean that there are significant differences between genders in terms of attitudes towards play. Our measure, however, was not successful in discriminating them.

In terms of the amount of time spent with and fun derived from digitally mediated content, the results were as expected. Males did report more digitally mediated play experiences than females did. The percentage of this sample that reported doing so, however, was smaller than expected. Further study should be conducted with representative samples to see if these percentages are the norm. Those who report engaging in digitally mediated fun/play activities appear to have a different relationship with computer technology than those who don't.

The findings appear to support the hypothesis that those who derive pleasure from computer environments are more likely to report higher self-efficacy in relation to computer technology. Technoplayers score higher on the technophilia index than non-technoplayers. Thus playing with computer technology appears to be related to feeling comfortable with and competent in terms of computer technology because play affects attitudes. The American Academy of Sciences report on women and science concludes that: "It is not lack of talent, but unintentional biases and outmoded institutional structures that are hindering the access and advancement of women". Although further study is needed to confirm these results, it seems probable that encouraging women to engage in more digital play will positively affect their relationship with computer technology. Given that many males start playing computer games when young, studies of younger age groups would be relevant to see how digital play affects attitudes towards technology in younger sample populations.

Engaging in challenging computer-based play environments that are considered to be fun (and perhaps useful) has a relationship to higher technological self-efficacy. Given that parents and educational and governmental institutions wish to increase technological self-efficacy among females, we recommend that females be exposed to complex digital play as early as possible and encouraged to invest time and money in this activity. Attitudes towards technology are formed at a very young age. Encouraging both genders to engage and play with technologically complex games will prepare them for a world in which science and technology are increasingly important.

ONLINE LEARNING

In this the trajectory of an online course in which graduate students collaboratively investigated and shared their personal experiences with respect to adult development is described. For this study, naturalistic inquiry was used to gain a holistic view of this semester-long course and to identify the specific emergent issues that characterized course dynamics. Using open, axial, and, to a lesser degree, selective coding, the following three issues were selected for further discussion: (a) flexibility of course to accommodate participants; (b) co-construction of meaning through the sharing of personal experiences; and (c) the expression of vulnerability and personal growth.

This course provided evidence that online courses can support deep learning about content, open sharing about personal experiences, and the development of a sense of camaraderie among participants. Students readily shared their feelings, critically examined course issues, extended their support in helping peers, and embraced many of the challenges of taking an online course. Implications are that benefits of online courses extend beyond the time and place independence they provide for participants, but also include the reflective and social environment they can foster. Additionally, in terms of developing environments to support interactivity, especially with respect to human-human interaction, it may be that less is more.

Over the last decade we have witnessed an explosion of the use of the Internet for supporting distributed education. The Internet, and specifically the World Wide Web (WWW or Web), creates exciting opportunities to make information available to large numbers of users residing at distributed locations and who work at different times. As such, there are numerous courses and even entire degrees being offered online-referring to those courses taking place by way of a computer network. One frequently cited reason for the development of these online courses is the increased availability of educational opportunities to users who, if required to be at a particular location (e.g., university classroom) at a particular time, would not be able to take the course.

Less frequently given as a rationale for these courses is that the learning climate that develops online is more supportive in terms of promoting reflection, intimacy and community than are those climates that emerge in the traditional classroom learning environments. In fact, it has been argued that course taken online are impersonal, superficial, misdirected, and potentially dehumanizing and depressing, with online courses actually disrupting the student-instructor interaction that creates a "learning community".

The online dialogue being examined in this study, however, suggests that students were willing to be vulnerable, were engaged in deep learning, and indeed felt a sense of camaraderie with their online collaborators. It is the goal of this reporting of the data to engage readers in the course trajectory, helping them to develop a contextualized understanding of the course experience and, in the process, a contextualized appreciation for the potential of online courses to situate learning and for contributing to personal growth.

While some researchers of online courses and distance education have taken the position that research in this area should focus on conducting controlled studies that can demonstrate cause and effect and result in predictive models, we are not arguing for a particular path to be taken in the development of online learning environments or even for a particular tool in this regard. In this online course only very simple interaction tools were used (e-mail, threa ded message boards, chats), with the focus being on using computers to support human-human interactions as opposed to human-computer interactions.

Two researchers studied a graduate level course focused on "the study of contemporary adult life with emphasis on the individual in the context of the field of professional practice of adult education". Using naturalistic inquiry and the constant-comparison method, the researchers examined all course postings and interviewed the instructor and a subset of students to develop a robust account of the course. We begin with a description of online courses, highlighting relevant previous research and then discuss this research in relation to adult education. A description of the research and course context then follows, illuminating three emergent issues that were central to, and framed, this reporting of the data. These findings are then discussed in terms of how the course design supported a sense of community, providing a backdrop for a broader discussion of the educational implications of online courses.

The need for providing learning experiences and supportive climates for adults is important in the increasingly complex and frenetic American society. Adults are challenged by new life patterns with multiple careers (and the transitions in between to negotiate) and with fewer stable social structures to rely upon. Adults are living longer and so are their parents, which bring additional stress at different points in the life span. As the past becomes less helpful as a guide to living in the present and more unreliable for the future, adults feel less secure about decisions and perhaps less confidence in their ability to make good choices from the bewildering complexity of career, family, and personal life choices open before them.

A central challenge for educators is to support the emergence of environments for adults to participate in their own learning with respect to those issues that are integral to their lives. A central goal of this research was to empirically examine one such online earning environment. Malcolm Knowles described a conceptual framework for facilitating adult learning 30 years ago with the exposition of his worldview perspective he labeled andragogy. In contrast to pedagogy, the teaching of children used in K-12 education, andragogy is based on the relationship between learner and facilitator in which it is the facilitator's responsibility "to provide a caring, accepting, respecting, helping social atmosphere".

Knowles described an andragogical design process for adult learning as characterized by seven elements. Pratt (1993) summarized the elements of the process: "(a) climate setting,

(b) involving learners in mutual planning, (c) involving participants in diagnosing their own needs for learning, (d) involving learners in formulating their objectives, (e) involving learners in designing learning plans, (f) helping learners carry out their learning plans, and (g) involving learners in evaluating their learning". The emphasis on andragogy is not, however, intend ed to imply that adults as opposed to children should be taught in this manner.

When adult education is discussed, it is not simply referring to education that brings adults up to some chosen mark of formal schooling; instead, it is referring to educational experiences that are intentionally designed to address adult issues, needs, and strengths. Although our theoretical perspective has much overlap with other learning theorists, highlighting Knowles' (1984) seven elements of andragogy illuminates important themes that have characterized much of the adult learning literature, and illuminates the pedagogical commitment of the instructor who taught the course being researched in this chapter.

While not all adult educators accept the distinction between pedagogy and andragogy, many agree with Knowles emphasis on the freedom of the adult learner to become a more self-directed learner and autonomous individual, and the power of the human agency to overcome social structures and individual circumstances in pursuit of learning to effect life change. In fact, and consistent with other learning theorists, it is our belief that all learners should be encouraged to become more self-directed learners. However, learning and motivation are not constructs residing solely in the mind, and we argue that human behaviour should be described in terms of a reciprocal interaction among individual and environment. Since learning occurs as part of a social, physical, and cultural context, the learner acts and is acted upon by the envir onment.

A central conviction underlying our perspective is that learning is a social act best supported through collaborative interplay among human beings-an interplay that can be effectively supported through the use of tools. This view of learning is consistent with Lev Vygotsky, who considered meaning to be a cultural construct and who argued that learning is a social process involving collaborative activities. The social environment is central in providing alternative views and other information that individuals can use to test the viability of their understanding and in building the body of propositions that constitute "knowledge."

Savery and Duffy argued that, "collaborative groups are important because we can test our own understanding and examine the understanding of others as a mechanism for enriching, interweaving, and expanding our understanding of particular issues or phenomena." Therefore, an important goal for online learning is to suppor t learners in making their ideas public, providing opportunities for them to build and refine meanings based on their own experience and that of their peers. While the introduction of innovative and complex technical structures can support educationally useful human-computer interactions, the focus of this research was on building a story of what can happen when technology is used to support human-human interactions.

• In contrast to traditional "delivery" models of education frequently associated with correspondence or mass communication models of distance education, current visions of web-based instruction and computer-mediated communication support more "participatory" models of education. In these participatory learning environments, students are not receivers of someone else's information and imposed meanings, but instead are actively involved in the creation of their own understandings and meanings. It is toward the development of increasing participation, not simply information dissemination, that many online courses are now directed.

Online education can involve both synchronous (real time, e.g., chat groups or video conferences) and asynchronous (e.g., discussion groups, mail groups) communication, as well as one-way informational postings (articles, documents, videos) that can serve as objects for supporting interaction. There has been much discussion with respect to the "technical" dimension of distance learning. However, less often discussed is the equally important "human" or social dimension to these environments? The focus of this research was on this social dimension, and it is this aspect that is highlighted in this brief discussion of online learning environments.

Those who are skeptical regarding the potential of web-based instruction to support robust interaction are usually referring to supporting both social and instructional interactions. Skeptics believe that web courses will not be able to duplicate the perceived social attributes of face-to-face instruction, or the adaptive interaction with instructional content that an effective teacher can encourage during face-to-face instruction. However, there has been much research that has found cognitive achievement of online, distance education to be comparable with traditional education, and in some cases superior to it. It is the contention here that computer-mediated communication tools create new opportunities for distance education courses and have the potential to facilitate increased instructional, as well as, social interactivity.

With respect to research regarding synchronous interactions, there has been some research suggesting less overall interaction in text-based than in face-to-face communication. However, research comparing asynchronous interactions with face-to-face interactions has found more promising evidence of robust interactions in asynchronous text-based communication. In fact, many educators have suggested that asynchronous computer-mediated communication actually promotes reflective and critical thinking due to the fact that it allows time for reflection and revision of postings that are perceived as having more permanence than the spoken word. The interactions can be of a more open and personal nature due to the "anonymous" feel of text-based communication, adding a social component to class dialogue.

In one study, Mikulecky carried out an exploratory examination in which he characterized the student discussion of web-based and campus-based adolescent literature classes. In general, he found that both courses had high degrees of student participation, addressed practical teaching problems, linked class content to personal experience, and made links among different class materials. With respect to differences, Mikulecky (1998) concluded that: "in addition to engaging in lengthier and arguably more thoughtful discussion, web-based students seemed to get to know one another better and treated one another with more warmth and dignity than did students in other contexts". He credited the lengthier and more thoughtful discussion to the fact that students could pause and reflect and refer to other resources before responding.

He also hypothesized that the "staring faces of 20 classmates can limit self-disclosure, and the adamant face of someone speaking a strong opinion can discourage others who m ight disagree". In a research study conducted on a graduate-level, computer-mediated course, McDonald and Gibson (1998) combined Henri and Rigualt's (1996) content analysis model for analyzing computer transcripts and Lundgren's (1977) model of group development as a basis for devising a coding scheme to examine course interactions. A primary focus in this research was to understand the percentage of postings that were interpersonal, and the types of interpersonal communication.

Findings suggested that 50-75% of course postings were interpersonal with postings coded as solidarity (giving or offering help, show of affection, warmth, liking, trust, closeness, unity, or cohesiveness) or as openness (expressions of feelings and self-disclosure) constituting 60-90% of all interpersonal postings. Further, the three different groups they researched were remarkably similar in the linear trends of group development over time, indicating a potential pattern of group development.

When they compared their findings with those models and findings described by researchers examining face-to-face interactions, they concluded "that people meeting, discussing, and collaborating as a group via computer conferencing have similar interpersonal issues, at comparable stages and proportions, as reported in the literature for face-to-face groups". In addition, participants formed cohesive, functioning groups with affection, measured as openness and solidarity, found to be central to their interactions throughout the course.

In our study, rather than focusing on coding percentages of interactions with respect to particular categories, the focus was on examining the overall course trajectory and on using naturalistic inquiry to identify and situate for the reader the central themes that characterize course dynamics. What make these findings of interest are the depth, quality, and intimacy of course interactions, and the fact that they all occurred as part of text-based online communication.

The course setting was a graduate-level computer-mediated course taught in the Fall of 1998. The class consisted of 34 students, 23 female and 11 male, ranging in ages from 27-56. Most were taking the course as part of the requirements for obtaining a master's degree in Adult Education. About one-fifth of the course participants had no prior exposure to the technology used in the course, another fifth were extremely technology competent (i.e., were using the Internet as an everyday part of their work and personal life), and the remaining students had limited computer literacy and web-browsing experience. Several students were beginning a graduate program after a long hiatus during which they had been working or raising a family.

The course environment was set up entirely as an online Website that was password-protected and included nine separate areas each consisting primarily of a threaded, online discussion board: Course Homepage, Announcements, Calendar, Syllabus, Questions, Discussions, Readings, Roster, and Help. The course was arranged in chronologically progressive steps to be completed by the course participants. These steps, called modules, were assigned specific time periods within which course participants would engage in activities for that particular module and ranged from topical discussions to the posting of online articles and URLs.

There was an initial meeting and a closing meeting in which students communicated using a video-based conferencing system. Aside from these two video-based meetings, all formal course contact took place using the asynchronous and, less frequently, synchronous conferencing tools. The course conferencing tools included a threaded message board and a chat space, both of which were created for this course. The Course Homepage provided a brief overview of the course objectives and provided links to the eight course modules. Associated with five of the modules were threaded, group discussion areas in which all students could share their work, and for Module Three there were eight small group discussion areas and one entire class area where they would share the outcome of their small group work.

These modules defined all course expectations, and the discussion areas and seven available chat areas constituted the virtual spaces where interaction would occur. The instructor in the Announcements message board posted any changes to these expectations. In addition to the discussion groups associated with each module and the Announcements message board, there were also two other virtual spaces where asynchronous discussions occurred. The Questions space was a message board where students posted questions to be answered by the instructor or other students, with 85% (over 100 postings) being answered by the students.

If participants preferred to ask questions in a private setting, the instructor invited questions via electronic mail. There was also In The Hall, which was a "general discussion area" where students made 122 postings about topics including assignment questions, technology concerns, off-task socializing, and posting of various resources. Also important to note was the Roster area in which student pictures and biographies were posted.

Central to the instructor's pedagogical commitment, and consistent with notions introduced by Knowles (1984) and other adult educators, the course was designed to support the participants in becoming more self-directed learners in which they took responsibility for their own development and change. An interesting and unique feature of this course was the interrelationship between the course content and the circumstances of the participants taking the course. In this way, there was much overlap between the course "content" and the course "context," with the participants studying adult development and learning as they were experiencing the same phenomenon.

In one student's words, "We are a study in adult development ourselves! In this class, I could read Hudson [an adult development theorist], reflect on my own life, then go to class or a chat, and see others in different situation." Also consistent with notions central to adult edu cation, the course was designed to be flexible and to support participants in the investigation of issues and the building upon experiences particular to their own lives. Briefly, those assignments that relate to presented data are overviewed. The course began with students posting autobiographies in module one, followed by URL reviews of three sites and the completion of a personal learning contract with the instructor. Students were then expected to complete a timeline assignment in which they filled in a posted timeline with their own personal events, and read the first chapter of a book by Hudson,

The Adult Years: Mastering the Art of Self-Renewal. In this opening chapter, Hudson relates an emotional story in which he discusses being paralyzed as a child and what he learned from that experience. Throughout the chapter, he interweaves his abstract conjectures about the process of adult development with case examples to illuminate, among other topics, notions of embracing change and notions of age as they relate to adult development cycles. It was the timeline assignment and chapter one of the Adult Years that served as the focal point of the second module discussion. In o ther modules, they posted and discussed individually selected research articles and books they read, had small group discussions around group projects, and in the last module they posted course reflections. In addition, students also had a final assignment in which they carried out a research project, which could be presented and submitted in various forms.

For this study, primarily naturalistic inquiry was used to gain a holistic vision of the semester-long Adult Education course. At a general level, the goal of the research was to develop a rich account, thick description, of the course happenings. Two researchers who were not involved in the teaching or grading of the course examined class assignments and took notes on the readings to better understand and trace course content through the discussions. Computer conferencing, with the automatic archiving of course transcripts, provided a rich data source with over 1000 individual messages. With the exception of two video-conferencing meetings, private electronic mail exchanged between participants, and some portions of the live chats, all interaction among course participants was recorded in the transcripts.

Although we examined archived discussions after the course ended this process involved immersion in the course activities over the semester, reading all class postings, and completing the assignments so that we might gain an "insider" perspective" on the course experience. We found in the research meetings that, similar to class participants, this participation changed our understanding of adult development in general and the understanding of our own development in particular. Therefore, in describing the data, we interject our interpretations, which came to serve an important part of our course analysis. Our member checks with students and the instructor suggested that reading the postings and completing class assignments did provide us with a "feel" for course activity, group dynamics, and the perceived sense of community among class members.

Meetings between the two researchers, the course discussion groups, researcher notes, student assignments, and interview data were used to develop what the anthropologist Clifford Geertz (1983) referred to as an "experience-near" perspective on course activity. Rather than imposing pre-existing hypothesis on the data, our interpretations were grounded in the data and systematically worked out in relation to the data. Through this process, the data and the emergent hypotheses interact in a dialectic fashion, reciprocally informing and being informed by the other, and allowing us to develop heightened sensitivity to the research issues. During the research meetings, we deconstructed our own assumptions, developed audit trails, and verified the credibility and trustworthiness of the interpretations.

The process of data analysis began with the entering all of the data into the qualitative software package, NUDIST, a database program that allows the researcher to code, analyze, and sort chunks of text based on emerging categories defined by the researcher. The analysis proceeded through three stages-open coding, axial coding, and, to a lesser degree, selective coding. Open coding refers to the process in which the multiple sources of data are "fractured," broken down, and grouped by similarities into categories of related phenomena. Consistent with the constant comparative method of analysis, this process involves asking questions of and making comparisons among the data and the theory to generate emergent categories.

The next step, axial coding, involved combining the categories from open coding in novel ways to (a) identify category characteristics, (b) develop propositions about category connections, and (c) identify the central phenomenon or core cate gory. This process involved applying a "coding paradigm" and checking, testing, and verifying the analyses through shifting back and forth among the existing data and the collecting of more data, posing additional questions, and refining hypotheses. Guba and Lincoln (1983) described this as a "hermeneutic-dialectic process." In their description, it is hermeneutic because it is interpretive in quality and dialectic because it seeks a Hegelian synthesis through a process of comparison and contrast of divergent views.

Continuing the hermeneutic-dialectic process, selective coding involves moving beyond the presentation of static codes to understand the contextualized process in which the coded incidents occurred. This process, in which the theory is made dynamic, allows us to determine why a particular incident "occurred, what conditions were operating, how the conditions manifest themselves, and with what consequences", allowing us to develop an appreciation for the process of learning in this particular course.

In this discussion, we began the selective coding process, however, much of that level of analysis and theory generation process is part of our ongoing research in which we have just begun examining subsequent iterations of the course to test and saturate emergent theories. In this reporting of the data our goals were more conservative, focusing primarily on open and axial coding with the intention of developing an empirical account of course dynamics and providing evidence that t he identified themes occurred.

Although our focus was on "what" occurred, in this examination and presentation of the data we do move beyond the presentation of static and abstract codes, contextualizing our categories for the reader in terms of the events through which the identified issues emerged. More specifically, we identified what we perceived to be significant themes and then traced their development over the course, sharing the data, our interpretations, and the importance of the data more generally. In triangulating these interpretations we examined multiple sources of data (class discussions, artifacts produced by course participants, required readings, and interview data) as a means of increasing the credibility of interpretations derived from naturalistic interpretations.

THE HERMENEUTIC-DIALECTIC PROCESS OF IDENTIFYING PATTERNS

Given that it was the intention to track "knowing-in-the-making" and not simply students' final summaries, grounded categories from the data were generated first and then we traced the historical development of a particular category (technical understanding, perspective on life development, discussion surrounding the birth of two course members' child) over the entire semester. Open coding of the 1027 class postings resulted in the identification of 53 unique categories. From here, the process of identifying the core course issues, axial coding, involved applying the hermeneutic-dialectic process to identify the central themes cuffing across these 53 emergent categories.

Two researchers examined the 53 codes and the associated postings looking for common themes. Once each researcher identified common themes, they were then discussed until both researchers had complete agreement in the category synthesis. This involved developing category descriptions, examining additional examples, and then revising category descriptions and adding new data until each node had been tested and sorted into a particular emerging category.

This process can be thought of as analogous to how the quantitative researcher uses squared multiple correlations to identify underlying factors, with common codes and associated postings being combined based on shared attributes. However, this process was different from factor analysis in two important ways. First, the overlapping variance was not a computerized calculation but was based on human interpretation and discussion as examples were compared to evolving category descriptions.

Second, unlike factor analysis in which factors are hypothesized to cause the particular items, we view the emergent issues as reciprocally defining and being defined by the particular categories. Said another way, the emergent issues and the categories stand in dialectic relations with neither having ontological status over, or previous to, the other. From the original coded 53 categories, axial coding led to the identification of three emergent issues that were central to the course experience and that have changed our way of thinking about the potential of online courses to support learning.

It is important to note the methodological rigor from which these issues were identified and substantiated. Although in this chapter we simply present a subset of the 1027 examined class postings to contextualize the identified issue for the reader, each of the three emergent issues was associated with a minimum of 183 class postings, all of which were more than three sentences in length. It is also important to note that the over 1027 course postings were not the result of one or two enthusiastic students, or because of course requirements-students were only required to make six postings.

Approximately 84% of students posted 25 or more times, 38% posted 50 or more postings, and 13% posted over 100 times. With respect to the emergent patterns, three issues for which we will present supporting evidence for their occurrence in this course are:

- The flexibility of the course to accommodate participants with varying backgrounds and interests (183 postings)
- The co-construction of meaning through the sharing of personal experiences (232 postings)
- The expression of vulnerability and personal growth by participants (386 postings)

The results section is presented in terms of contextualizing the reader in the course trajectory as it relates to each of the three emergent issues that characterized much of the course experience. With an eye towards understanding the emergent issues, it was not the explicit focus to examine pretest and posttest changes in student acquisition of content knowledge.

Instead, the focus of this reporting of the data was on capturing the course trajectory, of which learning was an essential feature. While interviews with the instructor and examination of final projects clearly suggested that deep and meaningful learning took place, the focus in this reporting of the data was to understand and illuminate issues related to course flexibility, co-construction and contextualization of meanings, openness, and the emergence of a sense of community.

EMERGENT ISSUES

In the results section, the three emergent issues identified through the data analysis process are discussed. The goal in this section was to use samples of the data to illuminate and contextualize the particular issues that were identified. For each of these three issues these data samples were selected from the 183-386 course postings that were coded as associated with that particular issue.

It is important to note that many of the postings were complex and loaded on more than one issue, and in this presentation of the data we frequently selected examples because they allowed us to illuminate the maximal amount of categories in the least amount of journal space-using examples under one issue that clearly have association with another issue. In presenting each of these issues, we arranged example postings chronologically so as to allow the reader to participate in the course trajectory. Although some researchers have pointed out that "calendar effects" influence activity patterns in online courses, this research focused more on the content of the online interaction than on features of the interaction itself.

An important component of the course story was the flexibility the course afforded class participants. This flexibility pertains not only to aspects of the course itself, but provided an opportunity for the participants to personalize course assignments, negotiate shared meanings with one another, and accommodate participants with varying backgrounds, experiences, interests, and goals. This notion of flexibility in the course was evident in the class members' autobiographies, the learning contract, the book reviews, and in the final project. Beginning with autobiographies, the instructor provided an opportunity for the participants to get to know each others' backgrounds and interests.

The participants were asked to write one or more paragraphs about themselves and submit a photograph to be posted on the course web site. In post interviews, students continually told us that this initial posting created a sense of openness and collegiality that continued throughout the course. This section was of particular interest to the researchers because it gave us insight into the backgrounds, experiences, interests, and goals of the participants and thus allowed us to track the inclusion of these aspects in the participant's projects and discussions.

Finally, evidence of the intimate and transformative nature of the course is captured in the instructor's final posting. Everyone has shared in the intellectual AND caring aspects of this community. Thank you all for helping me learn more about and to trust this process ...This has been an important learning experience for me as we make this transition to web-based courses.

The largely asynchronous delivery mode of the course provided freedom and flexibility in dealing with the constraints of resources such as time, space, money, and personal and family relationships. Freedom and flexibility was apparent in the fact that students developed individual learning contracts with the instructor, selected the theorists they would research, and in the diversity of group projects. The facilitator was also instrumental in setting the climate, especially in the conceptual framework of the learning activities and the tone of communications from the beginning. In fact, seven of the eight students who reviewed a draft of this chapter as part of our member checks, suggested that we had not adequately highlighted the importance of the instructor in creating a warm and open learning environment.

A second emergent issue in this course involved the co-creation of meanings as participants contextualized the course content in their personal activities. Having these online collaborative spaces served two purposes: contextualizing course activity in personal experiences and supporting the sharing of multiple perspectives. This is important when one acknowledges that the meaning of a concept or theory is not an objective property but is instead a situationally determined phenomenon, whose particular attributes are contextually dependent.

Toward developing an appreciation for the multiple applications of a particular theory, the ability to share and reflect with others who have had rich life experiences becomes essential and was a major asset of this course. We observed, the continual sharing of varying perspectives that contributed to the emergence and evolution of deep and grounded understandings, providing participants with opportunities for critical reflection that is not necessarily av ailable or, at the very least, taken advantage of in the traditional course classroom-especially when there are 34 class members. A central impetus underlying this reporting of the data, and the third issue, was to show how the online discussions provided evidence for students' willingness to be open and that this sharing led to personal growth.

For many of the course participants, course content was life content and life content was course content. Said another way, there was no meaningful separation between learning course content, participating in class dialogue, and who they were as individuals. This last notion, of personal development co-evolving with course participation, is a central notion that has been discussed by researchers examining learning as-part-of-a-community. Whether or not students' appreciation of these meanings will be more robust and will transfer to future contexts is beyond the scope of this reporting of the data. However, we expect that the personal significance and the contextualized nature of these understandings are more likely to transfer to other contexts than would content "acquired as coldly cognitive facts."

Four design/implementation components that contributed to the depth and intimacy of course activity were identified. First, the course structure was clearly flexible, allowing for class participants to adopt course work to issues that were of direct concern to the students, not simply to the course instructor. Second, the selection and order of course assignments were particularly conducive to the creation of an open and warm atmosphere. For example, the opening prologue and first chapter of the Hudson book was deeply personal, intermixing theoretical content with personal experiences, including a personal account of the author's battle with paralysis.

As educators, one frequently begins courses with assignments that are meant to create a strong conceptual framework for the material rather than creating a strong affective climate that can be leveraged for purposes of motivating engagement and supporting deep personal processing of the material. Educators need to invest in resources for developing course clim ate, not simply understanding of course content. Third, the gentle and non-intrusive facilitation of the instructor supported a warm and open learning environment. This point was emphasized by seven of the eight students who provided member checks on the earlier article drafts and something that was clearly evident in the examination of the course postings. Fourth, the language of the syllabus, interviews with the instructor, and our examination of the data indicated that the instructor was explicitly intending to establish an online learning community, as opposed to simply using the virtual space to post pre-determined content.

IMPLICATIONS

Contrary to the notions of those who consider computers as harbingers of the dehumanization of education and as contributing to the break-down of the student-teacher relationship, we found that computer-based, asynchronous tools can buttress learning in profound ways. The findings here have provided evidence that there emerged a positive, caring, and non-threatening environment for participants to learn about adult development in general and their own development in particular.

More specifically, it was asserted that course participants shared personal material, supported each other in addressing individual needs, and encouraged the evolution of thinking about course issues in a personal way. Consistent with other findings, students readily shared their feelings, critically examined course issues, extended their support in helping peers, continually posted even when it was not a course expectation, and embraced many of th e challenges of taking an online course. These findings suggest that benefits of online courses extend beyond the time and place independence they provide for participants, but also include the reflective and social environment they can foster.

We contend that asynchronous, computer-mediated communication tools actually promote reflective and critical thinking, allowing for deep and meaningful learning to occur. Consistent with those arguments advanced by other researchers, it is the authors belief that this is partly due to the fact that asynchronous text-based communication fosters the ability and opportunity for students to reflect on, and revise, their work. Obviously, this will not happen in all online courses. In this course, the instructor was committed to fostering a sense of community, and chose texts and assignments that facilitated deep and personal sharing (i.e., the Hudson textbook, the timeline activity, the autobiography assignment).

Further, the topic of the course, adult development, directly related to issues that were near and dear to each of the student's personal experiences. Therefore, the links between what was considered course content and what was considered personally meaningful were natural and, to some degree, expected. However, given that all interaction happened online, the fact that these links and the nature of the conversation were so deeply personal and seemingly transformative was not expected. It appears that at least for this particular application, the online discussion space fostered a personal experience for individual class members as well as for the class as a whole.

Open and selective coding was used to develop a grounded account of course dynamics, providing empirical support for the claim that online courses can support deep learning about content, open sharing about personal experiences, and the emergence of a sense of community. This is not to imply that all online courses, especially those involving less personal content, will foster deep and personal sharing. The emergence of such experiences is not an inherent feature of the technology per se, but arises from the confluence of the technology, student motivation and commitment, course assignments, and the content of the course. Technology simply provides educators, and researchers, with a powerful tool.

These findings do, however, indicate that deep and personal sharing is possible online.

Another important implication of this study was the importance of "staying out of the way" with respect to the design and use of computer-mediated environments. It seems that as environments with features designed to increase the interactivity that the tool can offer are developed, we may actually be adding noise to the free flow of interaction between course participants. The increasing ubiquity of computer mediated interactive environments adds urgency to this quandary. Instead of aiding in interactivity, it may be that each of these features serves as a filter. Less, it may turn out, is indeed more!. The more the technology can get out of the way, the more actual interactivity might take place in the environment.

In this online course, only very simple interactive tools were used. Participants did not interact with computers; they interacted through computers with each other. There were asynchronous message boards, chats, and some e-mail. Without the distraction of having to become proficient with new tools (ironically designed to facilitate interactivity), course participants were afforded the opportunity to leave behind the constraining shackles of learning a new technology. In this way, we are moving from a focus on human-computer interaction towards environments that truly support human interactivity. In other words, the focus was not human-computer interaction but human-human interaction as mediated by computers (Barab, in press). Should not the decentering of technology be the educational technologist's ultimate goal? Do more technical layers of innovation actually hinder "human" interactivity?

It is our responsibility as educators to investigate how we can use tools (i.e., the Web) to impact the educational experience. In this context, the tool not only supported student learning but also our ability as researchers to learn from their experiences. Online courses provide researchers with an exciting research opportunity in that they can capture significant portions of class activity, allowing for the reporting of "thick" descriptions of knowing-in-the-making. This chapter further provides researchers with a framework for characterizing online courses.

A significant piece of the overall online story was the instructor's and the students' willingness to embrace change, both in terms of the content of their discussions and in terms of the medium through which they were learning. There is a story about a man who was put to sleep in 1600 and wakes up in the 1990s. He looks at skyscrapers, cars, airplanes, computers, and hears radios and televisions and is amazed. Then, someone shows the man a college classroom where the professor is standing in the front of the students and delivering a carefully rehearsed lecture, and he knew it was higher education. We as educators must embrace change, not as passive observers or didactic sycophants. Instead, we must jump in and explore this new world, critically examining how it can help us improve teaching and learning.

In many ways, this course situated these notions for course participants by providing them an opportunity to experience change and their own ability to cope with it as part of their learning experience. In our rapidly changing technological society, students and educators must learn to embrace change. This course provided an example of a learning environment designed to support students in experiencing change, in understanding adult development as a process of change, and in engaging in the critical reflective process so necessary to benefit from and to encourage change.

It is through these types of experiences that educators can situate student learning about adult development and societal change, providing the field and the learner with new models for potentiating the teaching and learning process. This chapter provided empirical evidence for the existence of deep and meaningful learning in online courses, and it is the responsibility of future researchers to develop the grounded theoretical explanations of why and how.

Theory generation with respect to "why" and "how" online courses can support deep and meaningful interactions is part of our future research agenda. This process will require the examination of subsequent iterations of the course to test and saturate emerging theories, examining why the themes identified in this research "occurred, what conditions were operating, how the conditions manifest themselves, and with what consequences". It is then that we will be able to state not only that deep and meaningful, collaborative learning can occur online, but, more importantly, there are interventions that one can do to increase the chances that it will occur.

6

Hypermedia Learning Environment

Using the Experience-Sampling Method flow experience, 60 subjects were assessed three times during a one hour interaction with a hypermedia learning environment in an experimental setting. Two task conditions reflecting different depth of processing were introduced: scanning, covering a large area without depth and browsing as a fully elaboration of a system. Three indices of learning performance were assessed: (a) content knowledge, (b) structural knowledge, and (c) transfer performance. It was predicted that flow was the dominant state, flow should appear independent on task conditions and learning should be improved. Results showed that most of the users go into flow.

A detailed analysis of experience characterized flow as an optimal state of experience. All variables measuring the quality of experience were more affected by flow than by other contexts (i.e. fear, apathy, boredom). Flow experience was stable over the experimental conduction. Learning was not improved for subjects in flow. Results and some limitations are discussed with concern to motivational design of hypermedia learning environments and suggestions for future research are made.

Hypermedia is defined as a nonlinear representation of interconnected information units, such as text, speech, graphics, animated graphics, and video clips. As multimedia refers to the integration of more than one modality, hypertext structures enables that links are provided between these objects, both textual and graphical. Because of the great facilities hypermedia bears on the production, editing and recording of information, educators and technicians ascribe great potentials. Hypertext and hypermedia are proposed as the textbook of the future and allows for flexible information and training tools.

LEARNING WITH HYPERMEDIA

In considering the effect of learning with hypermedia and computer-based instruction, researchers have been concerned with several issues: the usability design, acceptance, cognitive processing of hyper-documents, and instructional design. The aim is to find out, how to best individually assist learning demands, cognitive learning stiles and to foster self-regulated learning. Several guidelines for good didactical and technical design of interactive multimedia were developed. In the discussion of hypermedia as a computer-based medium for learning, several aspects had to be considered.

One aspect of learning that repeatedly was stressed concerns the motivation of the users. Motivation plays at least two different functions: first, motivation is a prerequisite for the learner to approach training offers. This intrinsic interest may be caused by task characteristics, such as perceived autonomy and meaning. Second, motivation refers to maintaining users to interact with the tasks in the contexts of exploratory learning. Although the presentation of the material and interactive functions should be motivating and encourage the user to learn and actively search for information, little research on motivation in media use was done.

The need to recognize the motivation in instructional design has been advocated by Spitzer (1996) who claimed that learning environments should foster intrinsically learning motivation. Systems should be inspiring people to use it to evoke perceptions of pleasure and foster involvement. In vocational contexts it is shown that people with an intrinsic interest in a theme learn more independently, persistently, and profoundly. Consequently the learning performance should be increased.

AFFECT AND PERFORMANCE

Additional support for the relationship between motivation and learning is drawn from industrial and organizational research. Individuals in positive affective states have been found to be more creative, more helpful, better negotiators, and more persistent on uncertain tasks. Several studies collected evidence that affect state can predict employee performance. For example Staw, Sutton, and Pelled (1994) found that positive affect could predict not only performance, but salary and social support. Wright, Bonett, and Sweeney (1993) could show a positive relationship between dispositional measures of well-being and work-related performance.

However, this relationship is mainly given for dispositional affect, like optimism, depression, and other dispositional measures of well-being. Recently, Wright, and Staw (1999) found pleasantness-based dispositional affect strongly predictive of performance evaluations, whereas activation-based affect did not predict rated perfor mance. Due to methodical problems, the conclusion may not be drawn, that transient positive affect did not improve performance because performance ratings often reflect several months of previous employment. In this study affect state, being less stable and enduring over time, is matched with a continuous assessment of behaviour during human-computer interaction.

FLOW

One approach to investigating the motivational effects during media use is flow. Flow is a state of experience, which is characterized by an experience of intense concentration and enjoyment. Under the flow state, people become absorbed in their activities. Moreover, because the flow state is enjoyable, people strive for the experience. Following the trait/state debate, flow can be considered as a transient state of mood. The appearance of flow was proven in a variety of domains, including work settings, leisure time, human-computer interaction, and clinical symptoms.

Although the great majority of flow experiences are reported during working activities, people were overall more motivated in leisure than in work. Flow-like situations occurred more than three times as often in work as in leisure time. In general, challenging activities contributed to flow. Examining positive psychological states in the daily life of a sample of working women, Haworth, Jarman, and Lee found both work and leisure were important for positive psychological states and was associated with internal locus of control. Using a linear structural relationship modeling analysis flow was determined by the individual's sense of being in control and the level of challenge perceived in task interaction.

The Experience-Sampling Method (ESM) was used to evaluate the common experience of situations. Typically, subjects report their experiences following an arbitrary signal. Given the tasks they actually fulfill, and a description of the situation, ESM allows for the analysis of interactions between personal and situational variables. The frequency of experience sampling varies between five minutes and some hours. Studies showed that convergent and test-retest reliability of ESM was highly satisfying.

Direct comparisons with methods like time budget have ESM found to provide valid information. The main problem grew out of the fact, that ESM is more a heuristic than a standardized method emphasizing that ESM should be adapted to the aims and settings of research. Originally, flow was assessed through a description of the individually daily experience and related to activities, thoughts and so on. More and more the experience within a situation or a class of similar situations was evaluated.

FLOW IN HUMAN-COMPUTER INTERACTION

More specifically, the development and efficacy of flow on human computer interaction has been investigated. According to Trevino and Webster (1992) "flow experience in human-computer interaction incorporates the extent to which

(a) the user perceives a sense of control over the computer interaction, (b) the user perceives that his or her attention is focused on the interaction, (c) the user's curiosity is aroused during the interaction, and (d) the user finds the interaction intrinsically interesting". They found that, within computer interactions, flow consists of three dimensions: (a) control, (b) focus of attention, and (c) cognitive enjoyment (a construct comprised of curiosity and intrinsic interest that were highly interdependent). Moreover flow experience was associated with perceived characteristics of the software as well as with relevant work-related outcomes.

FLOW AND LEARNING

Some studies investigated the appearance of flow in learning environments. In a three-year longitudinal study, the relationship between emotional experiences and characteristics of the learning context in vocational school and company education was investigated with the Experience-Sampling Method. The experience of autonomy, competence, and social relatedness was related to contextual factors. Schiefele and Csikszentmihalyi compared the effect of different motivational factors on experience in school. In accordance with expectations, it was demonstrated that interest was a significant predictor of the experience of potency, intrinsic motivation, self-esteem, and perception of skill.

In an extensive five-year study on the development of talent of teenagers, Csikszentmihalyi, Rathunde, and Whalen showed among a diversity of factors that engagement with a talent was enhanced by the association of optimal experience with talent-related work. Recently, Chen investigated flow experience during web navigation. Chen et al., used an online questionnaire. Web users in the flow state were less likely to have a clearer goal than those not in the flow state. To date, relatively little is known about the motivational states and experiences of users while interacting with hypermedia systems. Investigations on flow in hypermedia learning system are still pending.

The purpose of this study was to examine if and to what

extent flow appeared during learning with a hypermedia system. Additionally, the flow state can be used as an indicator for a relation of perceived challenges and skills: flow appears when a balanced relation between the perceived challenges in the environment and the person's own capacity to act (skills) exists. Finally it is of interest if flow leads to performance improvement. More specifically, the following were hypothesized:

Hypothesis 1. Researchers have shown and suggested that human-computer interaction can facilitate the occurrence of flow. Moreover, the hypermedia environment of the Web may provide Web users with flow. It is predicted, that the use of hypermedia leads to a flow experience. More specifically, flow should be the most frequent experience, compared to other challenges/skills-contexts, like fear, apathy, and boredom.

Hypothesis 2. In flow theory, nine dimensions are specified that are related to flow experience: (a) clear goals, (b) immediate feedback, (c) personal skills well matched to given challenges, (d) merger of action and awareness, (e) concentration on the task at hand, (f) a sense of potential control, (g) a loss of self-consciousness, (h) an altered sense of time, and (i) experience which becomes autotelic. The first three dimensions are called the antecedents describing situational factors of the activity itself for reaching the flow state.

Merger of action and awareness, concentration on the task at hand, and a sense of potential control describing the experiences, that is, characteristics which are perceived during flow state. Finally the loss of self-consciousness, an altered sense of time, and experience, which becomes autotelic are effects focusing on the effects after entered the flow state. Following this argumentation, it is predicted, that flow experience is independent on lea rning conditions (depth of information processing), like information or understanding.

Hypothesis 3. Flow experience should increase positive work outcome (learning result). Individuals in flow are supposed to have a higher learning performance compared to individuals in fear, anxiety, and boredom.

Subjects were 60 students that agreed to take part in a study of hypermedia learning. The sample included M.A. students in business science (18.3%), jurisprudence (13.33%), organizational psychology (38.33%), and other faculties (30.04%). It could be suggested that all Ss were motivated to participate due to relevant themes. The ages ranged from 19 to 35 years, 55% were male and 45% were female. Subgroups did not differ in sex, age, or marital status (F [less than] 1).

MATERIAL

A hypermedia learning environment for the training of managers in management by objectives was used. It consisted of six modules dealing with (a) basics (definition of concept, elements and processes, concepts of leadership), (b) conditions of application (conditions of success and failure, efficacy), (c) techniques (goal definition, agreement on goals, performance assessment, coaching), (d) case-based test (Case study), (e) knowledge test (declarative, procedural, and transfer knowledge), (f) references and further materials.

Two short modules introducing the content structure and the interaction modes were proceeding. Nodes were represented at a four-level structure: (a) modules, (b) chapters, (c) sections, and (d) units. The levels differed in the extent of detail: whereas chapters contained the main aspects and an overview, units covered detailed descriptions of single aspects. Overall, the six modules encompassed 234 pages with three videos, six animations with spoken text and four graph ics. Users may navigate through the buttons "Next," "Back," and "End," or through the information button that leads to an overview of all pages with a mark on the actual page.

PROCEDURE

Subjects(s) were arbitrarily related to one of two conditions. In the information condition, Ss were asked to inform about the topic of the system. It was assumed that a nonelaborated surface strategy was applied under this condition. In the understanding condition, Ss were asked to work in more detail, because they were told that they would subsequently be tested by a knowledge test. Before hypermedia interaction, a baseline measure on content knowledge, activation, and affect was done. Following an introduction in the use of the system, all Ss had about 45 minutes to learn the system. After this interval they were asked to visit modules four (test of transfer performance) and five (test of content knowledge). Finally, a structure formation technique was applied to measure structural knowledge. The whole experiment lasts about 120 minutes.

In this study, psychological states were assessed by the Experience-Sampling Form (ESF), a self-report questionnaire that took about two minutes to complete. Items concerned affect (happy, cheerful, sociable, friendly), activation (alert, active, strong, excited), cognitive efficiency (concentration, ease of concentration, self-consciousness, clear mood), and motivation (wish to fulfill the activity, control, feeling involved) measured on 10-point Likert scales. We obtained self-reports from each participant four times. Subsequent to the first assessment before the interaction (baseline), experiences were assessed three times-15, 30, and 45 minutes after hypermedia interaction. It took about 1-2 minutes to fill out the ESE. The ESF includes items asking about the quality of experience, current experienced challenges, and experienced skills.

Quality of Experience

Quality of experience was measured by 14 items. Subjects were asked to rate the quality of experience using 10-point scales ranging from not to very high. Four questions referred to the subjects' perceived activation: strong/weak, active/passive, alert/drowsy, and excited/ bored. Four questions referred to the subjects' perceived affect: cheerful/irritable, sociable/lonely, friendly/hostile, and happy/sad. Two questions referred to the subjects' perceived concentration. First, "How well were you concentrated?" and second, "Was is hard to concentrate? Two questions referred to the subjects' perceived activation. First, "Were you succeeding in what you were doing?" and second, "Were you satisfied with how you were doing? Finally two questions referred to the subjects' motivation. First, "Do you wish you had been doing something else?" and second "How important was this activity to you?"

Challenges and Skills

According to Csikszentmihalyi and Lefevre (1989) the balance of challenges and skills four contexts were defined: in flow context both challenges and skills are greater than the respondent's average. In anxiety context, challenges are greater than the respondent's average, and skills are less than his or her average. In boredom context, challenges are less than the respondent's average, and skills are greater than his or her average. Finally, the apathy context was given if both challenges and skills were below the respondent's average.

Learning Performance

The learning performance was measured by three indices. First a multiple-choice questionnaire with 20 items was applied before (baseline) and after the session measuring the factual knowledge improvement. The maximum score to reach was 40. Second a structure formation technique was applied to assess the relationship between the set of concepts or knowledge units. A set of 32 concepts of the domain and eight relations was given to the Ss and they were asked to sort the cards in the right manner. A reference structure with 76 of 188 reachable points served to assess the performance. Due to high complexity of the structure, 76 points were valued as a good result. Third, transfer performance was measured by a case story that was given to the Ss and was asked to answer 8 multiple-choice questions. The maximal score to reach was 11.

ANALYSIS

Differences in the affective dimensions (Z-transformed) were tested with univariate analysis of variance. Associations among dependent variables were tested with the Pearson product-moment correlation. Variations in the quality of experience were assessed with multivariate analysis of variance for dependent measures. Finally, frequencies were tested with a chi-square test.

RESULTS

Descriptive Statistics

A comparison of the overall means of affective dimensions revealed that activation (M = 4.26, s = 0.81), affect (M = 4.28, s = 0.88), concentration (M = 5.11, s = 1.52), satisfaction (M = 5.03, s = 1.31), motivation (M = 5.09, s = 1.45) were medium-sized. Male and female participants did not differ in any of the affective dimensions (F [less than] 1). The stability of the responses ranged from r = .48 (p [less than] .01) for the activity-item (active versus passive) between time 2 and 3 to r = .90 (p [less than] .001) for total affect scale between time 1 and 2.

In accordance with previous studies all five dimensions are stronger in flow compared to fear, apathy, and boredom. Analysis of variances showed main effects on all dimensions, except on affect: on activation (d′ = 1.09) between flow and anxiety (F (3,56) = 4.1; p [less than] .01), on concentration (d′ = 0.97) between flow and anxiety (F (3,56) = 3.41; p [less than] .05), on satisfaction between flow and anxiety (d′ = 1.67), flow and apathy (d′ = 1.13), and anxiety and boredom (d′ = -0.99) (F (3,56) = 13.89; p [less than] .001), and on motivation (d′ = 1.08) between flow and apathy (F (3,56) = 3.34; p [less than] .05). However, there were no significant differences on the affect dimension in any challenges/skill-context (F (3,55) = 1.64; n.s.).

With the exception of motivation and affect all of the five dimensions considered where highly positively correlated.

FREQUENCY OF FLOW CONTEXT

The next question we addressed was whether flow is the most frequent experience, compared to other challenges/skills-contexts, like fear, apathy, and boredom throughout the use of hypermedia. Flow is the predominant context in users experience. About a third of subjects get into flow. Even flow is the dominant state, no significant differences between the four contexts were found ([Chi.sup.2] = 3.07; n.s.). Individuals' momentary affective states may be due to those before entering hypermedia interaction. To address this issue, we examined participants' initial activation and affect. Analysis of variances showed a significant decline in affect (F (3,56) = 3.38; p [less than] .02) and a similar tendency in activation (F (3,56) = 2.46;p = .064).

FLOW AND DEPTH OF PROCESSING

The second hypothesis proves, that flow experience is independent of learning conditions (depth of information processing), like information or understanding. The frequencies of flow experience does not differ between the two conditions ([Chi.sup.2] = 0.37; n.s.).

FLOW EXPERIENCE AND LEARNING PERFORMANCE

Three indices of learning performance were used to assess learning performance: (a) content knowledge (CK), (b) structural knowledge (SK), and (c) transfer knowledge (TK). In order to control for prior content knowledge, the increment in content knowledge was used as a dependent variable. Subjects motivated in flow were compared to those motivated in apathy. Although subjects motivated in flow reach higher scores on all three knowledge dimensions (CK: 27,6 (s = 21,8); SK: 61.7 (s = 18,4); TK: 8,7; (s = 1,2)) compared to subjects motivated in apathy dimensions (CK: 21,4 (s = 12,6); SK: 56.7 (s = 19,2); TK: 8,3; (s = 1,4)) none of the differences reached significance (F [less than] 1). In comparing subjects in flow to those in all other states this pattern of results was confirmed.

There was a highly significant correlation between prior knowledge and learning performance, not only for the absolute increase (r = -0.78) but also for the relative knowledge increase (r = -0.86). Overall: users had a significant increase in content knowledge after using the learning system (23 %). For the test of relation between the flow state and user characteristics a dummy coding was done. None of the correlation between flow and socio-demographics (experience with PC, experience with learning systems, experience with the internet, prior domain knowledge) was significant (r [less than] .10), indicating that the appearance of flow was independent of any of these user variables.

DISCUSSION

The purpose of this study was to examine the affective states in hypermedia interaction using the flow concept. Flow, as a state of optimal experience is not only a strong measure of transient affective state, but moreover may serve as an indicator of an appropriate task and level of complexity. First of all, and consistent with flow theory and prior studies, data show that activation, concentration, satisfaction, and motivation were the key factors that resulted in the state of flow. Subjects in flow reported significant higher levels on these dimensions.

Differing from flow theory, the dimension of affect was not significantly higher in flow, even the score was the highest compared to the other contexts of anxiety, apathy, and boredom. This may be explained by the task structure: usually learning tasks go along with high effort, and a medium state of affect. Possibly, the appearance of flow dimensions differs in relation to the tasks. The dominant approach in flow theory is to show that flow is unique for all tasks. However, future research should concentrate on the differences using a variety of tasks or classes of similar tasks.

Flow was not related to user characteristics such as prior domain knowledge and experience with computers, internet, or learning programs. Additionally, no differences between men and women were found in the core experiences dimensions, indicating that flow is a unique effect. Results indicating that the overall pleasantness of hypermedia interaction was high: over 30% of users got into flow, a state that remained highly stable during the session. This result is supported by Chen, Wigand, and Nilan, showing that about 25 % of Web user's reported flow state.

This is noteworthy because it shows that without taking user variables (skill and aptitude) into consideration; a third of the users can reach a highly motivating affective state in hypermedia interaction. To our view, this is meaningful; because it shows that learning systems can be designed that motivate users to use it. Nevertheless results show no relationship between flow and learning performance. This is contradictory to results and assumptions of other studies. Csikszentmihalyi and Lefevre, for example, assumed that flow strengthens the personal capabilities with the likelihood of learning new skills. However, two limitations of the present study must be taken into concern.

First, data show that all participants had a significant knowledge increase after hypermedia interaction. This means, that flow may facilitate the learning performance, yet at the same time, the other contexts did not hinder learning. Second, baseline measurements in previously knowledge revealed that participants had a high initial knowledge score. This ceiling effect may be the cause for the marginal increases in knowledge. Two improvements for further studies are recommended: the difficulty of the test should be increased or using novices with little prior knowledge. In order to increase ecological validity, this study was undertaken with g raduate students in a training lab but should be replicated with employees in an organization.

The major methodological limitation of flow lies in its dependence on self-reports. This limitation is particular in ecological settings, where inaccuracy and incorrectness of answering the questions may distort data. The experimental setting allows for control of these effects and the experiences could be validated by the ongoing observation. After completion, most of the participants told that they were highly satisfied with the system, had fun, and experienced a challenge in interacting. Flow theory explains behaviour and experiences in terms of situational variables, emphasizing the role of task context rather than individual differences in explaining human motivation.

This study followed this line of argument although personality factors may have had an additional significant impact on perceptions and experiences. For example, effects of cognitive styles and spatial abilities of users on learning performance has been found in using multimedia. In summary, this study showed that the application of flow theory to hypermedia learning-environments can be a sensitive technique to assess system design features. Rather than just evaluating the technical aspects, it can be used to assess motivational design aspects during the learning process.

The motivational perspective of instructional design has important implications for user-centered design and from a marketing point of view. For example, if we are able to determine the variables that may support to entering a flow state, we could develop a strategy for improving the changes of user consummation. Moreover, implications for organizational learning could be drawn. If people reach the positive feelings that go along with hypermedia learning and find satisfaction in hypermedia interaction, they search for such situations, not only in work but even in leisure time. This is highly desirable from a self-regulated concept of learning that emphasizes the active role of users' not alone in learning but in seeking learning situations as well.

THE ORIGINS OF ANALYTICAL CARTOGRAPHY

A single academic paper that leads to a whole theme, sub-discipline, or even a paradigm, within cartography is clearly a remarkable thing. Tobler's paper has been cited many times, and sequels to the curriculum presented have been proposed that define analytical cartography by its subject content. Of more concern here are analytical cartography's origins, its institutions and Tobler's unique contributions. Recent intellectual re-scoping of the geographic information systems (GIS) field has given us definitions of geographic information science and geo-computation. The pivotal role of the technology of GIS in transforming contemporary mapping science and geography has been discussed at length. Few would doubt the depth of this transformation, and other sub-disciplines of geography, including critical theory and human geography, have now entered into the intellectual dialog defining the discipline.

Analytical cartography is a sub-discipline of cartography that lies behind much of the development in geographic information science. Analytical cartography has been described as "the solid bedrock of theory upon which the field of geographic information systems is rapidly building". More specifically, analytical cartography "deals with the theoretical and mathematical background behind cartography and the rules cartographers employed in the mapping process". Some common elements of definition include the use of mathematical principles and techniques, the part of cartography independent of a specific map-making technology, and the use of the transformational view of cartography proposed by Tobler, extended theoretically by Moellering and refined by Chrisman.

Analytical cartography is wholly integrated with spatial analysis within geography, and Tobler himself links work in migration, population, interpolation, and map projections under this common approach. Despite Tobler's own varied links to quantitative geography, analytical cartography from the outset dealt with the formalization of the discipline necessary for the digital transition, already well under way in government cartography, but less so elsewhere.

In Tobler's paper of 1976, we are told that traditionally, cartographic education in American universities involved making maps by hand. "One knows, a priori, that all maps which can be drawn by hand can also be drawn by computer-controlled devices". One knew, of course, because it was already being done that way in the government world of military and intelligence mapping, in what has become to be known as the "codeword mapping community". Academic cartography was necessarily playing catch-up at the time with the advances of two decades worth of intensive, but deeply secret, analytical cartography.

This gap between academic and clandestine analytical cartography was, however, one of degree and not of a kind. The mathematician Robert Hamming noted, famously, that "the purpose of computing is insight, not numbers". Tobler made a corollary statement that "the purpose of analytical cartography is the development of geographical theory, not the inventorying of geographical phenomena." Tobler's straightforward definition of analytical cartography is distinctive, but in reality it has been difficult to separate theoretical advances from mundane applications, both in the practical and historical context. Data and theory interplay always, whether the data involved are classified or not.

The purpose of this chapter is to examine the social context of the early years of analytical cartography, to expand upon the influences that shaped analytical cartography (and therefore also GIS) and to examine what role analytical cartography should play in the ever changing playing field of computer-based spatial information. We will examine the following questions: (1) what external influences shaped the early growth of computer mapping and analytical cartography, particularly with regard to their role in advancing Tobler's shaping of the discipline; (2) how can analytical cartography's inherently interdisciplinary nature support institutions and infrastructure for the future of the field; and (3)what are some of the theoretical concerns and research issues that will influence the next generations of computer mapping systems?

THE SOCIO-TECHNICAL ENSEMBLE OF ANALYTICAL CARTOGRAPHY

Analytical cartography was born into a world much different from today's. When Tobler's 1959 paper "Automation and Cartography" was published, America was gripped by the threats, both real and imagined, of the Cold War. This critical period in recent history is being increasingly seen as the pivot to explaining the modern history of science and technology, especially in information science. Recent studies in the new field of Science and Technology Studies often focus on what they call the "socio-technical ensemble" of a specific technology.

The implication is that no particular result of science in the applied sense is "invented" without context but, instead, is the result of seen and unseen influences from society at large via a group of "actors" who make the actual decisions and build the technology-the socio-technical ensemble. This technological systems approach was pioneered by Hughes

(1983) and involves consideration of the technological, economic, and political context of scientific and technological change. It is important to note that while all of the actors have been involved in the technological and scientific work, they may not have been aware of each other, each other's work, or their own role in the work. This was especially true of the deeply secret programs, where "compartmentalized" or "need-to-know" secrecy isolated the actors and their networks. We will pursue this theme, but focus generally on analytical cartography, and specifically on the contributions of Waldo Tobler.

Stuart Leslie (1993) introduced into the study of the history of science and technology the term military-industrial-academic complex in his work explaining the socio-technological ensembles at the Massachusetts Institute of Technology and Stanford University. This three-way model has been shown to apply extensively to the development of computing technology. In many ways, analytical cartography follows the same model, with the added dimension of the nature of the secrecy of the relationship, and the powerful degree of integration between the sciences and technologies involved in mapping. In prior work, we have proposed our own model for the flow of knowledge and expertise between institutions in the mapping science world.

Four major influences converged scientific attention on "automated cartography" during the formative period, which might be defined as the period between the end of World War II and the end of the pioneering CORONA satellite reconnaissance program in 1972 (and, coincidentally, the launch of the first Landsat satellite). The first of these influences was the legacy of the Second World War, but the others were solidly founded in the Cold War. The four influences were:

- German advances in analytical mapping methods before World War II;
- The SAGE computer-based control system for Early Warning radar;
- The DISIC camera and its integrated set of hardware and methods that automated the geo-rectification process of

imagery under the CORONA program; and

- The CORONA MURAL camera that added the analytical construction of three-dimensional terrain maps to the automated CORONA systems.

The first major component of the socio-technical ensemble was the recognition of the importance of WW II German advances in geographical science. Prior to the war, German and Swiss optical and precision mapping-related hardware was known to be of the highest quality. In the closing days of WW II, the Allied Powers discovered that the German war effort had made significant advances in geodetic control networks, in analytical photogrammetry, and in cartographic analysis. Map overlays were probably prepared on translucent media and overlaid manually for two different suites of applications. The first was map overlay use to solve problems in military operations, which probably included troop movement, trafficability, and terrain masking.

The preparation and use of these overlays were made part of routine procedure, thus forming the origin of the application of systems theory approach to geographic information. The second application was systematic regional-scaled planning for schemes for Aryan colonization in territories overrun by Germany, the secret General Plan for the East. Walter Christaller's Central Place Theory was integral to these planning efforts, and was, in fact, devised for this application. These applications may be the earliest and most significant of the various multiple origins of geographic information systems, or at least of map overlay.

The map overlays, and a vast quantity of other material, were discovered by teams of Allied intelligence officers and enlisted operatives (particularly) in the European Theatre toward the end of the war. Most significant and certainly the most geographically critical were the discoveries of the "Hough Team," a party of several dozen officers and enlisted men and women deployed under the command of Major Floyd Hough, later Chief Geodesist, Army Map Service. Hough's objective was to secure a broad array of maps, data, and disparate geographic technologies, particularly German analytical photogrammetric equipment, which was known or suspected to be superior to Allied technologies.

Near the small village of Saalfeld, however, the Hough Team discovered a cornucopia of geodetic data, either generated by the German army, or captured from other sources, mostly Russian. The materials captured by the Hough Team constituted a revelation to American military geographic institutions. In cartography, geodesy, and photogrammetry, the Germans had been decades ahead of the Allies. Most important of all, these geodetic materials were the missing link between the known datums and mapping of Western Europe and the "denied territory" of the Soviet Union. They later allowed accurate geo-referencing, mapping (and targeting) deep inside the Soviet Asian land mass.

The Hough materials remained state secrets for many years, yet they had a major impact on American cartography. While most of the geodetic materials remain classified or restricted even today, the data, equipment, and materials were systematically evaluated by government enterprises, including the Engineering Board of the Department of the Army, and summaries of these investigations, particularly with reference to photogrammetric equipment, were published in the cartographic and photogrammetric literature.

During the 1940s and early 1950s, dozens of academic papers discussing the German instruments and methods appeared. Knowledge of the methods clearly influenced GIS. For example, while not directly concerned with cartography, Ian McHarg, who later made significant contributions to landscape ecology using overlay analysis, served at the end of WW II as a translator and interrogator of captured German officers, occasionally with technical and scientific occupations, although he denies that this experience influenced his later work.

Many other prominent cartographers, geodesists, geographers and photogrammetrists made their impact in the practical and theoretical developments during this period, including Arthur Robinson and Frederick J. Doyle. The open and explicit nature of scientific progress in analytical cartography, which encompasses the many fields and disciplines often called the mapping sciences, changed significantly in 1958 with the start of the CORONA program. After that date, publications such as Photogrammetric Engineering began to feature either very generalized descriptions of technologies, or descriptions of what were called theoretical and future systems that existed in fact but were classified as top secret.

As the Soviet space and missile programs developed rapidly, the United States developed several secret technology programs aimed at redressing the balance of the Space Race. The remaining three influential factors in the socio-technical ensemble of analytical cartography arose during the period of technological response to the perceived Soviet threat. The factors can be characterized by three salient clandestine projects from the era: SAGE, DISIC, and MURAL. Their names are capitalized because that was and remains U.S. classified procedure for top secret programs.

Each of these programs accelerated the integration of computers and accurate geo-rectification into analytical cartography, bringing about the digital transition in cartography that Tobler discussed in the 1976 paper. SAGE pioneered global data acquisition and its processing and graphic display by digital computer. The DISIC camera on CORONA allowed automated geo-rectification to great accuracy of imagery taken from space, and the MURAL camera on CORONA introduced systematically geo-rectified stereo imagery and, thus, the third coordinate dimension into scientific, digital cartography on a global scale.

Among the responses to the Cold War air threat was an unprecedented early warning system including the Pinetree, DEW and Mid-Canada "lines" of linked radar stations. These systems required constant real-time operation in remote areas, and severely strained existing command, communications, and control systems. The Air Force's response was a massive command and control project called SAGE, based on the Office of Naval Research's Whirlwind computer. SAGE (Semi-Automatic Ground Environment) was a command-and-control system designed to warn of attacks by Soviet bombers. University and other research on SAGE pioneered developments in real-time computing and core memory use that eventually spread throughout the computer industry, in particular time-sharing operating systems.

Technical and scientific development of part of the SAGE system took place at the Rand Corporation in Santa Monica, California. SAGE required the ability to map incoming aircraft and missiles on a global scale on radar oscilloscopes. SAGE may have influenced analytical cartography directly. Waldo Tobler worked on SAGE at the Systems Development Corporation (SDC), an offshoot of RAND, from 1957 to 1958, after completing his MA in Geography at the University of Washington. While there, following an interest aroused by reading a paper on the Azimuthal Equidistant projection, he took a class in map projections from Richard Kao, a mathematician and expert on the topic from the University of Michigan.

While in Santa Monica, Tobler built upon computer experience learned in William Garrison's classes at Washington, and at SDC he was exposed to computer-driven plotters at a local electronics company. The paper "Automation and Cartography" was written at this time; this was his second paper on the topic, an earlier version having been published in the German cartographic literature. Tobler's role on SAGE was to generate graphics and plastic overlay templates for radar screens that were used in simulations for training radar operators to respond to emergency situations. Often the maps were manually generated, but the use of the Duplexed IBM 704 led to experiments with computer mapping and plotting directly.

Tobler's later academic work toward a Ph.D. reflects this influence yet is outside of the early warning radar systems context. "Tobler later linked the map projection research directly to analytical photogrammetry, via the work of Tissot.

According to Tobler, "Tissot's results are completely general and can be applied to aerial photographs, to radar images, or to camera lenses". The importance of projections at the time was unmistakable. Arthur Robinson's first edition of the cartographic classic Elements of Cartography contains a 54-page chapter on "The Employment of Map Projections," including a more thorough coverage of Tissot's theorem than is currently common.

While SAGE drew upon a large number of cartographers (analytical and otherwise), it was another top-secret program that led to the first degree of systems integration necessary for true geographic information science. In 1958, the officially secret but publicly acknowledged Air Force experimental space reconnaissance project WS-117L was officially cancelled, but, in fact, it was reconstituted at unprecedented levels of government secrecy and renamed the CORONA project. CORONA's role in pioneering successful space flight, satellite reconnaissance, space technology, systems integration, and recovery of film from space has been well documented elsewhere.

Absolutely critical to CORONA was an alliance between the CIA, industry and academia. Contractors worked extremely closely with the CIA and Air Force on CORONA. Academia often also played a pivotal role, particularly Harvard and Boston Universities and the Ohio State University. Considerable linkages between the actors within the network of participants show up in academic circles. For example, the Harvard University Optics laboratory, which had worked on bomb sights during World War II, moved to Boston University when Harvard demilitarized its campus after the war.

From the Boston University laboratory, Richard Leghorn and Walter Levison helped design and develop the series of cameras that led to the KH or Keyhole series for CORONA. In 1957 Leghorn and Levison co-founded the Itek Corporation from the Boston University Optics Laboratory, and went on to build cameras for CORONA and other programs. Leghorn was later Chief of Intelligence and Reconnaissance Systems Development at the Pentagon, and he is the originator of the

"Open Skies" concept. Thus the same individual working on the same technology area went from the military, to the academia, to industry, and to the intelligence world within the CORONA project.

From an analytical cartographic standpoint, CORONA led to three major technological and scientific break-throughs in mapping. First, when the initial satellite images successfully revealed Soviet military bases, space launch pads, and air defense systems, it was quickly realized that existing American maps and geodetic controls were too inaccurate to wage or prevent war by ICBM. This perception accelerated ongoing research by the geodetic and mapping agencies of the Department of Defence (DOD) to produce a Figure of the Earth suitable for the nuclear age.

A major component of the effort built on the unique resources in photogrammetry, cartography, and geodesy assembled at the Ohio State University. Faculty and staff there had been mobilized for military research and training for the Second World War, and, in the post-war period, the university became a major center for research on Cold War geographic challenges. A crash program to minimize the problems of geodetic control involved sending hundreds of CORONA technicians and scientists to Ohio State, where a Ph.D. program in geodetic science had been constructed to build the science base in geodesy and photogrammetry for mapping Asia and doing image interpretation from CORONA and other imagery.

Another breakthrough was the design of two remarkable mapping cameras, the ARGON and DISIC, which were pivotal to CORONA. Incredibly enough, the Hough team's captured German and Russian geodetic materials provided a critical link between the European and Asiatic datums, which involved a re-discovery of ruined survey towers on the Trans-Siberian railroad using CORONA imagery. The identification of these towers allowed first-order geodetic control to be extended across the great bulk of Eurasia-without setting foot on the "denied territory" there-an unprecedented achievement in the history of geodesy.

This and a variety of other important breakthroughs in electronic distance measuring devices, densification of global gravity data networks, and major advances in computational power, led to the important series of Earth-centered global datums that was a first stepping stone on the way to WGS 84 and the global positioning system (GPS) of today. CORONA's remarkable success placed a demand on the image rectification, co-registration, and geographic data management process. Mechanical, photo-electric, and, later, electronic technologies were developed for information management. Starting about 1966, the Dual Integrated Stellar Index Camera (DISIC) on CORONA (still classified even today) coupled a lower-resolution calibrated index camera with two stellar cameras, providing much tighter geo-rectification for CORONA.

DISIC was paired with improvements in automatic position correcting and spacecraft attitude adjustment systems, particularly the Universal Photogrammetric Data Reduction and Mapping System (UPDRAMS). UPDRAMS was designed to accept a wide range of mapping and reconnaissance photographic inputs, with emphasis on the reduction of covert satellite photography. The corrected data were run through automatic or semi-automatic map compilation programs, such as the Universal Automatic Map Compilation Equipment (UNAMACE) which produced rectified orthophotos, and the Automatic Stereo-mapper model 11 (AS-11) which produced rectified contours.

The couplings between the CORONA film, the DISIC system, UPDRAMS, and the UNAMACE and AS-11 created a mapping and geo-data system beyond the capabilities and purposes of the original CORONA reconnaissance mission. As the CIA noted, "Enhanced by improvements in system attitude control and ephemeris data plus the addition of a stellar-index camera, CORONA eventually became almost the sole source of DMAs military mapping program." These methods and technologies pioneered "automated cartography." Thus, previous projections of future developments in automated cartography published in the open cartographic literature were first realized, in fact, in the deeply classified world, rather than in the academic world.

With the success of the KH-4 "Mural" camera in 1962, CORONA returned stereo imagery. To the geo-rectification task already mastered was added the need to process overlapping imagery via a stereo model and to extract three-dimensional information about the terrain, buildings, etc. While the principles of stereo imaging had been understood for over a century, CORONA demanded systems that could provide both accuracy and rapid throughput. Once the analog equipment of the early CORONA program gave way to computer-assisted and eventually digital processing, new possibilities for using terrain elevation data became evident.

The need for an understanding of digital topography led to research outside of CORONA, much of it funded by the U.S. Army Research Office. Waldo Tobler later worked on terrain analysis methods, using principles from image processing that he had learned from Azriel Rosenfeld. As Tobler stated in Analytical Cartography, he "wished to emphasize that mathematical methods are involved, but also that an objective is the solution of concrete problems". One great concrete problem was in accurate topographic map production, and CORONA itself played a major role in topographic mapping at the United States Geological Survey and elsewhere.

Out of this work came the first space-based analytical photogrammetry (and cartography) of the stereo model and its derivation, and also the methods, equipment, experience and infrastructure for "industrial-scale" use of the data. Light stated "that the 'pixel concept' shows great promise for reduction of topographic imagery and information to usable, storable, retrievable, displayable form." The familiar Digital Elevation Models and Triangulated Irregular Networks evolved for these and earlier data types and became the basis for enormous digital "libraries."

The legacy of these pioneering programs includes contemporary national and global digital elevation coverages.

Light's metaphor of the "image of the world in a barrel," based on the nickname devised by the staff of the U.S. Army Topographic Command for a cylindrically shaped mass storage device, lives on a third of a century later in the latest concept definitions of the Digital Earth project. This brief consideration of the influences that shaped the origins of analytical cartography has focussed on the government as the motivator for change within cartography. Generally speaking, academic departments were slow to adapt to the new cartography, and the emerging field of GIS was even slower.

This may have been partly due to the fact that the first generation of graduates of analytical cartography found careers in government agencies, especially such mapping agencies as the Defense Mapping Agency and its separate predecessor service-level constituences, the United States Geological Survey, the CIA and the National Reconnaissance Office, rather than going into teaching and academic research. Tobler noted the "gap between official government cartography and academic geographical cartography".

Nowhere was this gap more evident than in the 1967 National Academy of Science's Summer Study on the potential uses of space satellites. This study, convened and funded by the National Aeronautics and Space Administration (NASA), was directed toward brainstorming "useful applications of Earth-oriented satellites." The list of the 112 participants is a veritable who's-who of the military/industrial/academic personnel of the era. Waldo Tobler participated, along with Frederick Doyle and Amron Katz (a pioneer CORONA camera designer), on Panel 13 of this meeting, writing a report on "Geodesy and Cartography."

As CORONA was in full swing at the time (and actually being used for the purposes proposed in the report, unknown to some of the participants), this section of the civilian NAS report was intercepted and classified as Top Secret, and so did not see the light of day until the 1980s. While in some cases the academic community was able to work creatively with the military and intelligence mapping community, through a complex system of knowledge sharing we have called elsewhere the "shuttered box", Tobler's observation on the separation was based on reality.

The driving force of digital transition in cartography (the computer) was at first poorly represented on academic campuses, and even then only in programs primarily in computer graphics and image processing. Geographic information systems were invented (or reinvented) in many different disciplines as computer software became more functional. Traditional academic departmental organization, along with parallel organization of research funding sources, worked to impede cross-disciplinary contacts to best exploit GIS. While some of these barriers remain, today the interdisciplinary nature of integrative research is far better recognized.

Similarly, each successive generation of software made the tools and methods more accessible and easier to use and teach with. By the mid-1980s, GIS had started its rise to primacy in geography departments and elsewhere, and analytical cartography was carried along as part of the theory so necessary to understand the tools and applications. Tobler's definition of analytical cartography provided the critical interdisciplinary linkages that were often missing in other technical fields of geography, and that were absolutely central to the classified systems.

The curriculum for Geography 482 at Michigan included coverage of remote sensing, image processing, computer cartography and graphics, spatial analysis, map projections, computer programming, GIS, and geodesy. While the history of analytical cartography remains to be written, many of the research challenges are as rich today as they were in the late 1970s. For example, automated extraction of cartographic features from imagery for direct placement onto maps- the automated feature extraction problem-remains to be solved, at least in the open literature.

Despite recent advances in automatic feature extraction, the inclusion of the human interpreter in the processing of spatial information remains essential. Training machines to duplicate human vision tasks has been the topic of vast amounts of work in computer vision, artificial intelligence and in some areas of graphics, such as text recognition and map labeling. Completely automated extraction of cartographic features in their geographic coordinate space remains as a holy grail for futuramic analytical cartography.

INSTITUTIONS OF ANALYTICAL CARTOGRAPHY

Analytical cartography grew few formal institutions outside of the classified world. Besides a few books, and many academic papers, journals in the field tended to either disappear (e.g. Geoprocessing), or fully integrate with GIS (The American Cartographer). Some important conferences and meetings were short lived, and never had continuity. Exceptions were the two conference series-AUTO-CARTO, the International Symposium on Computer-Assisted Cartography, and the Spatial Data Handling Symposium-of which only the latter survives. As issues related to algorithms and data structures moved from theory to application, the software development end of analytical cartography moved over to various professional conferences and publications series.

The professional societies built around an interest in analytical cartography that was central to the classified programs, especially CORONA. The American Congress on Surveying and Mapping and its member group, the American Cartographic Association, embraced during the 1980s and 1990s the broader context (and wider audience) of geographic information systems. Analytical cartography is very often alive and well in the University system but has changed name, discipline, or content to suit the applications orientation of GIS-what Tobler called the "popular title" of computer cartography. One could argue that this has led to a dearth of new research from academia on analytical cartography. For sure, most recent innovations have come from the software industry behind GIS (automated text labelling, object orientation, etc.), or from the government's role as the seeder of new technologies.

One could ask, without there ever being any formal institutions behind analytical cartography, does the field need any now? This can be answered in several ways. One model of knowledge production, the historically influential Vannevar Bush view of research, holds that pure research contributes to a "pool of knowledge" that can be tapped for applications at some future time. The CORONA experience and the methods for managing research pioneered by the Defence Advanced Projects Agency (DARPA) have clearly demonstrated that scientific progress can be forced forward rapidly when resources are concentrated on specific problems, and when initial failure is tolerated.

We now find ourselves in an era characterized by a pool of government (military and intelligence) knowledge that is being opened up only by intervention through government programs and exchanges, in particular the Dual Use program and activities under the Cooperative Research and Development Act, both of which primarily benefit industry and commerce. The concept of pure science as a "pool of knowledge" that applications can subsequently exploit has recently been questioned, yet it remains a versatile model. Analytical cartography, perhaps like some other scientific endeavors, suffers from the fact that much of the pool is "off limits."

The declassification of the historical remote sensing programs like CORONA, and the release of material under the Freedom of Information Act and other programs, have led to a reappraisal of the origins, motives and influences of post-war American science and technology. While the release of the CORONA imagery has proved to be a valuable resource for earth and environmental science, experience has shown that the technical documentation and research reports that accompanied the imagery were also invaluable to making the data useful to science, especially in directing a reappraisal of unclassified work that was contemporaneous with the black science, the so-called "black" or missing literature that forms the pool of untapped cartographic knowledge.

The CORONA declassification in 1995, for example, released over 38,000 pages of documents into the publicly accessible National Reconnaissance Office (NRO) archives and the National Archives. The prospect of the release of additional material, more up-to-date and therefore closer to the scientific agenda of today is excellent and, hopefully, has a great deal to offer the next decade of cartographic research. Another component of the intelligence/science community relations is the MEDEA Project. MEDEA is a scientific committee tasked to obtain vital environmental data from classified information collected by spy satellites and other sensors that could be instrumental in accurately assessing deforestation and other significant environmental problems, and identifying indicators of global warming.

The MEDEA committee has been influential in planning data acquisition for science, implying that future declassifications will provide an increased boon to academic research. These declassification efforts, therefore, have great value to analytical cartography and should be welcomed and encouraged by cartographic scientists. As commercial one-meter imagery becomes commonplace with the launch of ICONOS II in 1999, resolution restrictions that date back to the Cold War on the current intelligence systems will diminish by an order of magnitude.

Despite the earlier Cold War emphasis on progress in classified cartography programs, with the end of the Cold War, academic research and applications have assumed more central roles in the development of contemporary analytical cartography. A more appropriate model for the next decade might be three-way collaboration-between government, industry and the academia-or the Leslie model. This is obviously more important than ever without the over-riding dominance of national security so central to the Cold War. Some institutions are responding to this need. For example, the recent request for proposals from the National Imagery and Mapping Agency's NURI (NIMA-University Research Initiative) has involved collaborative identification of research foci of maximum mutual benefit, especially between the

Department of Defense (DOD) and the National Science Foundation (NSF).

While such collaboration between nominally civilian and military and intelligence agencies is far from the approach to government support of research envisioned by Vannevar Bush that led to the founding of NSF, it very much reflects the systems of knowledge production that emerged from successful experience during the Cold War. Neither should it remain unstated that such an approach necessarily involves both positive and negative dimensions for each of the involved parties. While clandestine collaboration had many successes within programs like CORONA, the path of progress was fraught with cost overruns, inefficiency and unproductive rivalries, not to mention the opportunity costs involved. Foremost among these costs may be the gap in the literature of analytical cartography.

The history of analytical cartography has been immersed in the government, industrial, and academic triad. We can now publicly acknowledge the central roles played by military and intelligence mapping communities in this ensemble. The newest major institution in the evolution of analytical cartography, which is the World Wide Web, is itself the product of previous collaboration by researchers spanning all these communities.

The Internet is a 'network of networks', and the original network, the ARPA-Net, was designed specifically to ensure robust and secure communications and data transfer during or despite nuclear war. The inherent utility of that network has now been demonstrated for other applications that span the planet. The World Wide Web for cartography has taken on the role of map librarian, map distributor, map publisher, and software provider. Having already led the way as a knowledge provider, the Internet map server technologies have made web-mapping a daily activity for many computer-literate Americans.

Beyond the present capabilities of the wired networks, the developments in mathematical theory and encryption algorithms that underlie progress in wireless communications and high mobility computing are likely to lead to another revolution in analytical cartography, the second of our lifetimes. The driving force this time will be commerce, and, hopefully, human welfare and economic and environmental sustainability. Driven by dual use-the military/civilian application of classified assets-and fed by the newly recovered "missing pool" of previously classified knowledge, the new analytical cartography will challenge human visual perception, involving complex spatial dimensions, web-telepresence, multiple simultaneous views, computer simulation, virtual and augmented reality, error-free navigation, and real-time field geography.

Just as CORONA's new view of the world spawned both a whole new science and an industry to rectify, integrate, register, cross-correlate, and convert images into information, the so-called ubiquitous computing will demand that cartography redesign the map from the bottom up into its own new geometries and reveal uses and applications undreamed of in our cartographic philosophies. As Tobler suggested, the technologies and representations will change with the new cartographic technology. Fortunately, as Tobler also noted, the principles and mathematics of mapping will remain virtually the same.

7

Globalization Approach to Web Privacy

Many observers in the United States relate the adoption of the Internet to a sense of erosion in domestic privacy and parental authority. Numerous books, academic articles, public opinion polls, and press reports (as well as solutions and regulations) alert Americans to the allegedly inescapable consequences of the introduction of an additional eye (ear/ mouth) into the home's technological environment. The tone of inevitability underlying the discourse about Web privacy in the United States implies that these concerns also carry over into other societies as the Web spreads across the world. Yet, while seemingly the ultimate metaphor of globalization, the Web is experienced locally by individual users embedded in particular families, cultures, and politics.

In what ways, then, do users' approaches to the Web derive from their "indigenous" cultural construction of the machine? Where do they draw on U.S. values and fears, as embedded in U.S. cultural and technological exports? Our purpose here is to suggest a framework for answering these questions by constructing the Web's global and local faces as a dialogue that is anchored within transnational political and economic bearings. By situating a society's cultural and technological practices within broad political and economic parameters, we can identify global forces and local voices, and study the dynamics of their co-existence.

As an exploratory foray using this approach, we present a comparative survey of U.S. and Israeli parents' attitudes toward the Web and Web privacy. The survey highlights the cultural specificity of information disclosure practices but suggests, at the same time, that global influences may be at work. As constituted, the data do not allow us to causally tie these complex patterns to particular extra-national influences. They do, however, help define the areas in which these influences might be fruitfully explored in future studies, and they point out the usefulness of bringing historical and geographical considerations to every level of Web research.

THE NEED FOR A GLOBAL SYSTEM PERSPECTIVE

Accounts of the global spread of the Web have tended to adopt two contrasting narratives. According to the first, technology's inherent features spark the same opportunities and challenges and so, the same concerns and meanings, for users around the world. The alternative narrative insists that technology-both the hardware and the social meanings that are associated with it-is socially constructed. Works that adopt the first, essentialist/universalistic narrative, assume that technology affects people and societies in predictable and inevitable ways.

Writing about privacy, for example, Garfinkle (2000) argues that "[t]echnology is not privacy neutral. The overwhelming tendency of technology is to out privacy. By its very nature, technology is intrusive". These works note that the Web's elementary hardware-computers, monitors, and network connections-can be seen everywhere one looks. The same holds true for the basic software-the browsers, search engines, chat rooms, and instant messaging systems that link millions of "surfers" worldwide. These works imply, therefore, that the whole world is exposed to essentially the same Web; and that effects, problems, and solutions inescapably derive from the technology, and are generalizable universally to virtually all locales.

Relativist works, by contrast, suggest that although the telephone, radio, and television, for example, have distinctive technological features, the social meanings and controversies around these features developed over time through elaborate interactions among various constituencies, value systems, and regulatory regimes. From this perspective the fluid, multilingual, and radically interactive Web, in particular, subverts any attempt to construe it as a fixed entity, as it allows for and indeed cultivates intertwined and mutually-constitutive relationships between medium, text, and consumers/audiences/ users.

In this way, relativist works introduce users into the study of the human-machine interaction and position them as active shapers, decision-makers, and producers of meaning. Significantly, they situate users within communities, in actual times and places. Thus, arguing for the embeddedness of ongoing human-machine interdependence, Livingstone (1998) emphasizes the significance of sociopolitical and economic context in relation to an important project on "young people and the changing media environment in Europe" that she helped coordinate:

> Contexts of media use are elaborated ... in two main ways. First, differences in social, cultural, economic and political structures both across and within European countries are likely to make a difference to children and young people's media use. Second, among western countries these structures are themselves subject to broader processes of modernization, processes which have particular significance for young people.... To the extent that different countries represent different positions on these broad structural variables, including the diffusion and appropriation of media, comparative analysis offers a kind of natural experiment for explaining the meanings, uses and impacts of new media within each country.

The Need for a Third View The technological-universalistic and constructionist-relativist narratives of technological diffusion and globalization, of cultural adoption and localization, are clearly incongruent and indeed mutually exclusive. It is interesting, then, that what is common to both is a reluctance to situate the human-machine encounters they explore in the context of transnational political and economic relations that underlie these processes. Thus, where essentialist thinkers privilege the Web's global impact with little attention to local contexts, relativist and comparative analyses similarly overlook the interplay of the local with the transnational.

Livingstone (1998), for example, practically rules out a cross-cultural research design in which countries are structurally interdependent or disproportionately influencing one another when it comes to new media. She argues that "to make ... comparisons [between countries] manageable in practice, the research should be restricted to modernized, western countries which are undergoing related sociopolitical changes; overlarge national differences would prevent observations interesting in one country being informative for another".

The upshot of this guiding principle is that the dominant interest in reporting the results of the European project is on cross-national comparison without cross-national influence. Thus, four of the five studies presented in a European Journal of Communication issue devoted to the twelve-country project headed by Livingstone (1998) treat the countries they compare as unrelated entities. They ignore the fact that many are geographically close to one another, many share languages and cultural products, and all belong to a European Economic Community that is developing pan-continental rules about electronic commerce, Internet privacy, and a host of other activities that affect life on the Web.

The one exception to this hermetic approach offers an account of globalization as a conflation of cultural practices. Yet it still avoids asking where the "global" originates, what forces lie behind its interpenetration of the local, and whether that interpenetration takes place differently in countries that have substantially different sociopolitical and socioeconomic environments.

THE UTILITY OF A POLITICAL ECONOMY OF CULTURAL GLOBALIZATION

In order to account for users' cultural constructions of technology and to make sense of their specific ideas about Web privacy, we must contextualize technological development and human practice within broad economic and ideological parameters. Both software and hardware play a major role in today's international trade. The economic relationships that develop in the world markets for such information products recall the division of nations into a political hierarchy of core, semi-peripheral, and peripheral nations that Immanual Wallerstein and others have employed for analyzing international domination.

The model proposes that certain economic actors (predominantly corporations), based in a few core nations or regions, hold determinant influence on both the disposition and the effective operation, as well as the output, of less developed peripheral and semi-peripheral parts of the world. This, in turn, "enables the extension of the authority of the economic and social model" encouraged by the core nations. Recent writings on globalization challenge the construction of international economic hierarchy as an explanation for the colonialist shaping of social actions and attitudes. Placing caveats on such linear reasoning, they raise important questions about the nature and direction of ideological influence.

Appadurai (1996), for example, insists on the subversive, local, and liberating potential of globalization for diasporic ethnics around the world. But the emphasis on the democratizing potential of global access runs the risk of overlooking the political economy of power. Such perspectives may thus underestimate the role that economic domination emanating from hegemonic nations or regions plays in framing local cultural ideas about what a particular technology should "do," how it ought to be distributed and used, and to whom it ought to be sold.

In an attempt to develop an approach to media technology that is sensitive to the interplay between global forces and local appropriations, we suggest a political economy of cultural globalization. Our perspective conceives of globalization as a dialogue between hegemonic interests and cultural practices, and uses the international economic and political power structure as a starting point for investigating transnational ideological influences. At the same time, it contextualizes and historicizes those local attitudes, practices, interpretations, and ideologies that assign culturally specific positions, roles, and meanings to technologies. As a result, it is attentive to the flows of influence from many directions, at many levels, and across time.

This dualistic approach is crucial when it comes to the Internet and information disclosure. By its very nature, the topic involves an intersection of global forces and local voices, technological facts and cultural choices. In political-economic terms, the Internet was developed at the core of the world system, among the wealthiest and most powerful nations. With significant European contributions, it evolved mainly in U.S. scientific establishments, originally for military purposes.

Core-country corporate Internet leaders such as Microsoft, Intel, AMD, and 3Com subsequently situated strategic outposts in parts of the world that reflect different positions along an innovation/cheap-labour continuum: Some nations (e.g., Finland, Israel, and India) are relied on for their ability to contribute cutting-edge knowledge about hardware and software. Other countries (e.g. Indonesia and Malaysia) provide inexpensive, stable, and compliant manufacturing conditions. Independent firms in all regions vie to provide the large companies with component parts as well as to export their own innovations to Web-linked consumers.

What is especially interesting about these relationships is that firms based outside the core often find it most profitable to create software and hardware that do not necessarily speak to their own cultural, practical, and ideological concerns. Instead, they address their products to their most prominent markets. Web privacy, security, and child surfing, for example, are topics that have generated huge investments by consumers and Web firms in the world's wealthiest regions. To participate in the revenues engendered by software and hardware tied to these concerns, industries at the periphery and semi-periphery of the western economy must keep up with debates regarding media policy and technological fixes that take place in front of U.S. regulatory agencies, the European Commission, and within English-speaking academic circles.

What are the implications of such globalizing tendencies for members of a non-core society when the values embedded in their major, core-oriented software and hardware exports do not resonate with their own local sentiments? For example, will members of a non-core society translate their traditional views on information disclosure into Web attitudes and practices even when they do not match the Web-privacy approaches that occupy global media and business interests? Such questions imply propositions regarding comparative research that are quite different from the ones that Livingstone posits about the comparison of equivalent, impermeable core countries. Here the emphasis is on sharply different socioeconomic conditions, on often-contrasting political and cultural circumstances, and, importantly, on international relationships and cross-influences.

THE CASE OF ISRAEL AND THE UNITED STATES

A comparison of attitudes between Israelis and Americans on Web-related topics allows us to begin deciphering the interplay of technology, hegemony, and the local construction of meaning. The positions of Israel and the United States within the hierarchy of the global system are strikingly different. In contrast to the United States, a continent-spanning nation of more than 300 million people with a gross domestic product of U.S. $36,200 per capita, Israel, with about 6.4 million inhabitants, has a GDP of U.S. $18,900 per capita.

Similarly, whereas the U.S.'s international economic and military influence places it unchallenged at the core of the world system, Israel may be considered outside that core. Despite the large share of knowledge-based export in its economy and in contrast to additional indicators of economic growth, Israel's troubled borders and state of occupation and the related military expenditure, as well as comparative measures of inequality relegate it to an intermediate position in the world system.

In spite of this gap, Israel is increasingly linked to the United States by high-tech relationships. Many U.S.-based multinational firms-Intel, Cisco Systems, 3Com, IBM, and Microsoft-have established foreign subsidiaries and R&D centers in the country. Moreover, a large number of indigenous companies are competing with an eye to creating hardware and software that can serve security, privacy, networking, and broadband needs in the United States and elsewhere. The Israeli economy has been intent on satisfying U.S. and European demands for high-tech and often Web-related products. As the partner in a major high-tech venture fund noted, "Israel is a very export-oriented country."

A computer industry recruitment site aimed at English speakers exemplifies the two-way flow between Israel and the United States, suggesting that although exports throughout the globe are the goal, a U.S. frame of reference is dominant. In mid-2002, the site noted that "like other high-tech centers around the world, the high-tech industry in Israel is directly impacted by the stalled U.S. economy." Nevertheless, it pointed out, "with some one hundred (mostly high-tech) companies traded in the U.S., Israel is second only to Canada in terms of foreign presence on U.S. stock markets." Consequently, "with the establishment of many American subsidiaries in Israel and the development of the internet in English, your mother-tongue is definitely an asset."

The mutual Israel-U.S. interest that we identify at the corporate and worker levels is crucial at the level of management. Israeli executives keep their ears to the ground regarding social as well as technological developments in core regions of the world (especially the United States, Europe, and the United Kingdom) with an interest in capitalizing on the needs that arise in these potential markets. From pioneering Firewall security software in the early 1990s to recent encryption products that address recording conglomerates' problems with Web-based copyright infringements, many home-grown innovations are heralded in the general Israeli press not for speaking to Israeli sensibilities but for expanding exports.

Newspapers' financial sections provide their readers with detailed reports about U.S. regulatory and advocacy debates about the nature and right to information privacy as well as parents' concerns about keeping their children safe from objectionable content and predators on the Web. These developments come up in discussions of new product possibilities, in the coverage of Israeli privacy violations, and in the typical reporting that goes on about things American. But the linkage with the United States is not limited to business interests. Growing fast, the number of Israeli surfers was a bit less than a third of the nation's homes in early 2002.

With relatively few sites in Hebrew available to them, Israeli users navigate to U.S. sites and communicate through U.S. applications, using software and hardware that (wherever produced) map onto U.S. ideology in general and concerns about privacy in particular. Moreover, films such as The Net, which enact U.S. information disclosure nightmares, are frequent television fare. Prevalent, too, are magazine and newspaper feature articles that translate U.S. concerns into local parlance. Israeli media have paraded U.S. concerns about digital information disclosure as at once prophetic of things to come and as being different and quintessentially American.

The foreign accent of the coverage of privacy issues stands out both in the close watch reporters keep on privacy developments-technological, legislative, and regulatory-in the United States (and to a lesser extent, Europe), and in the breadth and depth of the analyses that they provide. This detailed complexity stands in a sharp contrast to the scarce reports on privacy issues in Israel. Few and far between, the local stories speak to the essential confrontation between regulators' efforts to introduce standards of privacy and common counter-arguments in the name of national security.

The high-tech reporter of *HaAretz*, Israel's elite newspaper opined that most Israelis have not considered Web privacy concerns as relating to their society. He added that the press' conscious U.S. orientation on these topics reflects a sense that American judicial and legislative activities raise interesting conflicts and issues that might stimulate thinking in Israel, where legislative and judicial awareness of this area is undeveloped. The relative indifference to privacy violation that the press implicitly attributes to its audience is in fact in line with the collectivist strands of the country's founding ethos. Israel was established on an explicit socialist ideology in which individuals were firmly situated as members and partners in the project of nation-building, rather than lone adversaries of big government and centralized power.

The country was, and arguably still is, a "recruited society" in which the boundaries between the self and the collective, between personal needs and desires and national imperatives and objectives-and thus, between on- and off-stage and between public and private life-are difficult to outline. Further, while the country has witnessed strong pulls toward privatization and individualization during the past decade and a half, recurrent national threats appear to strengthen Israelis' commitment to the collective and reduce whatever centrifugal tendencies they may have temporarily entertained. Thus, when 15-year-old Ofir Rahum was kidnapped and murdered by a Palestinian woman he met through the ICQ instant messenger (just 2 weeks before the Israeli survey), newspaper coverage adopted the conventional framework of the Arab-Israeli conflict.

References to the danger of information disclosure on the Web were overwhelmingly subordinated to the discourse on national security. Structurally, too, personal privacy is treated differently in Israel from the U.S. Unlike Americans, Israelis must carry an official picture identity card. While an American driver's license and social security number may seem comparable to the Israeli ID, symbolically and functionally they are profoundly different.

Israelis' ID numbers identify them in most of their encounters with both government and non-government institutions (for example, medical and university authorities), and citizens over 18 are required to carry the card at all times; the use of the social security card, on the other hand, is legally, normatively, and practically restricted, while the driver license is, by definition, voluntary. Israelis cannot (or find it difficult to) reinvent themselves due to both the close watch of the Ministry of Interior (and the ID it issues) and the country's size; Israelis know each other.

Related to that is the fact of the army. While the myth of universal draft is no longer sustainable, it is nonetheless the case that by the age of 18, every Israeli youth can expect to be called by the army for pre-military examinations and checks. The results of the tests form the basis for the personal file that will accompany him or her in the years to come. Focusing on Israeli society alone, we might expect that these particular local circumstances would directly influence Israelis' attitudes about Web privacy. Yet, as we have seen, very different perspectives on information disclosure in relation to the Web appear on Israelis' media radar screen in discussions of U.S. (and, to a lesser extent, other international) business concerns and social reports about the Internet.

To what extent, then, do Israelis translate their relative tolerance for information disclosure offline into their computer privacy practices? Do they follow the hegemonic preoccupation with the Web's (inevitable) information leakage? Do they develop a construction of the Web that reflects their traditional information disclosure practices, or are these global and local influences blended in some way? In an attempt to gain initial insight into such intertwined transnational cultural interrelationships, we compared U.S. and Israeli views on the Web, gathered in surveys on Web attitudes that were conducted in the United States and in Israel.

THE SURVEYS

The U.S. survey was undertaken in early 2000, before this comparative investigation was conceived. That survey was a follow-up to a study conducted by the second author in 1999. The study was the first academic exploration of U.S. parents' attitudes and reported activities regarding the Web as it related to their children. One aim of the 2000 survey was to track differences from the previous year's findings regarding what parents were generally thinking and doing about the Web.

To do that, the survey presented parents with 14 statements about the potential benefits and harms of the Internet for children, which were asked in the original survey. It asked parents how much they agreed or disagreed with each of the assertions along a five-point scale; from agree strongly to disagree strongly. The survey's second aim was to explore an emerging issue. As teenagers were becoming major users of the Web, commercial sites were increasingly gleaning information from them for marketing purposes. The 2000 study asked how parents and youngsters (teens and tweens, a marketing term for 10-12 year olds) conceive of releasing information to Web sites and, if they regarded it as a problem, whether they wanted anything done about it.

The survey addressed the concern about the Web and the leakage of family information through 14 statements about privacy and the Web. Parents and youngsters were asked how much they agreed or disagreed with each of the assertions along a similar 5-point scale. Also included were scenarios aimed at comparing what the youngsters say would be acceptable for teens to reveal to Web marketers as compared to what their parents say would be acceptable for teenagers to reveal. Although the questionnaire was not created for use in cross-national comparisons, we realized that a Hebrew translation would offer a unique opportunity. For researchers interested in the cultural construction of the Web, it could provide an exploratory window on the extent to which parents in two countries have similar strong beliefs about the technology's benefits and problems.

And, from the specific standpoint of developing a political economy of globalization, we could note where Israeli respondents located themselves, when it comes to the Web, along the range between specifically "Israeli" and mediated "American" attitudes to information privacy. Roper Starch Worldwide conducted the research for the Annenberg Public Policy Center. Telephone interviews were conducted with a nationwide cross-section of 1,001 parents of children 8-17 in homes with Internet connections. The Random Digit Dialing (RDD) sampling methodology was used to locate respondents. During the interviews, parents were asked to answer questions while thinking about their child aged 8-17, who had the most recent birthday.

When the child the parent had focused on during the interview was at least 10-17 years old, an attempt was made to also interview that child. When that child was not available, another 10-17 year old child in the household was interviewed. Approximately half of the 304 children 10-17 year-olds that were interviewed were selected from the same households as the parents. The other half of the children's sample (for which parents were not interviewed) was located using the Random Digit Dialing (RDD) sampling methodology. All the interviews were conducted January 13 through February 17, 2000. Interviews with the adults averaged 20 minutes and the ones with the kids averaged 10 minutes.

The Israeli interviews were conducted by the Machshov survey firm one year after the ones in the United States (January-February 2001). The RDD and interview procedures used were the same as in the earlier study. The comparison, then, is between random samples of 1001 U.S. adults and 304 adolescents, and 1000 Israeli adults and 305 adolescents, who lived in households with online computer access and at least one child between ages 8 and 17.

THE SURVEY FINDINGS

The two samples of adults were similar on a number of basic demographic variables. In each sample, 41% of the respondents were male and 59% were female. The vast majority of each group (83% of the Americans, 85% of the Israelis) were employed. Similarly, around half of the parents (57% of the Americans, 55% of the Israelis) were aged 30-44;

almost all the rest (33% of the Americans, 44% of the Israelis) were aged 45-59. Most parents in each sample were married, though the proportion of married Israelis (92%) was higher than the proportion of married Americans (79%). Similarly, 50% of the Americans and 45% of the Israelis had college or post-graduate degrees.

It is impossible to know, of course, whether the similarities in these labels actually mask major cultural differences in what the labels mean. Certainly, the presence of two very different societies came through in the absence of "race" as a relevant category in Israeli society and its replacement by "country of birth" and "country of father's birth." In the same vein, answers about "household income" point to a very different scale in the two countries, as Israel's average income is substantially lower than that of the U.S.

In fact, the Israeli survey firm did not consider it appropriate to ask the American income question, which directly solicited the parent's family income bracket. Instead, the parent was told that the net average household income in Israel is 8,000 New Israeli Shekels and asked to state whether his or her household income was around that average, a lot or a little lower, or a lot or a little higher. Only 10% responded that they fell below the average, while 57% said they rose above it-an indication, albeit indirect, that the sample was substantially wealthier than the nation as a whole. The more "direct" U.S. question was elusive in its own way: Since 26% refused to report their yearly income, it allowed even less inference about the online families' socioeconomic standing. Those who did answer, however, reflected a group that was only somewhat wealthier than the nation as a whole.

Against this backdrop of similarities, differences, and the ambiguous meanings of both, one major difference stood out immediately between the two samples in relation to use of the Internet: While 94% of the U.S. adults said that they had personally used the Internet, only 64% of the Israeli adults reported that. Clearly, a much higher percentage of Israeli than American parents had bought the service for their children only. Among the Israeli adults who did report getting on the Internet, the perceived sense of expertise was similar to their U.S. counterparts.

Nevertheless, that a third of Israelis with the Web at home weren't users at all might suggest that these Israeli nonusers' privacy attitudes should properly be compared with Americans who don't have the Web in their homes. The 1999 study comparing the attitudes of U.S. parents in households with computers but with and without the Web at home found that the latter were somewhat more negative about the Web's ability to improve their children's lives. The 1999 study didn't plumb privacy attitudes, but it did lead us to wonder whether Israeli parents with the Web at home who have never used the Internet would be more concerned about privacy than those who have had direct experience with it.

Overall, the differences between the Israeli groups are small and not significant statistically. By contrast, the differences between the Israeli and U.S. samples are substantial as well as statistically significant. The answers from the U.S. and Israeli parents to the 14 statements about potential benefits and harms of the Web reflect very different mind-sets about the Web. U.S. parents hold strong opinions about its effects. Large numbers believe that it is a useful and even critical component of a child's education, and large numbers believe, often at the same time, that it gives youngsters access to content with "troublesome" values.

Substantial percentages of Israeli parents, by contrast, are much more skeptical of the technology. They don't believe the hype about its advantages and they don't accept the rhetoric about its dangers. Twice as much as U.S. parents, however, they worry about their ability to help their children navigate the new technology. For example, while 74% of U.S. parents agreed or agreed strongly that "children who do not have internet access are at a disadvantage compared to their peers who do have access," only 23% of Israelis answered that way.

In fact, on all of the "positive" statements about the Web, U.S. parents were far more likely than Israeli parents to agree or agree strongly. U.S. parents were far more prone to say the

Web is a safe place, that it helps their kids with homework, that their children discover "fascinating, useful things," and that it can help them "learn about cultural diversity and social tolerance." Israeli parents also tend to be mellower about potentially negative effects of the Web than are their U.S. counterparts. Almost half (46%) do express concerns about the Web's ability to interfere with family values-around the same percentage of U.S. parents expressing the concern.

Yet substantially smaller percentages of Israelis than Americans are concerned about the possibility of bad effects of specific Web content. Almost twice as many U.S. parents as Israelis (59% vs. 31%) agreed or strongly agreed that "going online too often might lead children to become isolated from other people." Similarly, 72% of U.S. parents were concerned over exposure to sexually explicit images on the Internet, as compared to 28% of Israeli parents; 62% of the U.S. parents, and 31% of Israeli parents were concerned over exposure to violent images. And, while 74% of U.S. parents reported that they were "concerned that children give out personal information about themselves when visiting Web sites or chat rooms," only 24% of Israeli parents agreed.

Israeli parents did say in substantially higher proportions than their U.S. counterparts (48% to 26%) that they "often worry" that they won't be able to explore the Web with their children as well as other parents do. That about half of Israeli parents had such a feeling of deficiency is interesting in view of the Israelis' self-evaluation of Web expertise, which was similar to U.S. parents, and their overall mellow attitude to Web effects. At the same time, Israelis' expertise with Web marketers was admittedly relatively limited. Only 25% of them, as compared to 60% of the Americans, reported that they have read Web site privacy policies more than once or twice.

Moreover, 53% of the U.S. sample indicated that they bought something over the Internet, compared to only 30% of the Israelis. We wondered whether these countervailing tensions that didn't show up nearly as much in the U.S. parent population-mellowness versus a felt deficiency, general expertise versus specific inexperience with marketers-would translate into clear cultural differences regarding the teenagers' release of family information to marketers.

What we found was more complex than these straightforward differences. On the one hand, a clear majority of both Israeli and American parents reflected the kinds of information privacy concerns that the Israeli press had, in fact, continually discussed as American internet privacy issues. On the other hand, the Israeli parents did diverge strongly from their U.S. counterparts along cultural lines with respect to naming who has the responsibility to try to solve these privacy problems.

RESPONSES ON INFORMATION PRIVACY

When it comes to the kinds of information parents say are acceptable for teens to give to Internet marketers, the differences between Americans and Israelis seem to be a matter of degree rather than of kind. Israeli parents were consistently more likely to agree that it was acceptable for a teenager to release certain types of information to marketers in exchange for a free gift. Yet for most categories, the percentages of both Israelis and Americans agreeing about the giving out of data were well under 40%. Moreover, about the same small percentage of parents (24% of U.S. and 20% of Israeli parents) said they themselves would answer a variety of personal questions to marketers in exchange for a free gift when it was given a cash value.

Clearly, then, Israelis' traditionally tolerant attitude toward information disclosure did not show through strongly here. Most people in both parent populations were uncomfortable about themselves or their offspring confiding family information to marketers. At the same time, for many of the statements, the gap in perspectives between the two populations wasn't that great (not exceeding 10%). Answers to several statements do, however, suggest that major cultural differences between the U.S. and Israeli respondents are also at work.

According to one finding, more American than Israeli parents (60% to 37%) confirm that their concern about Web privacy has increased since going online. Another finding indicates that substantially more American than Israeli parents admit being nervous about Web sites having information about them (72% to 52%). A third finding suggests one reason for the lower percentage of Israelis compared to Americans: A far smaller segment of the Israeli parents (54% to 31%) knows that Web sites collect information about them even when they don't submit information.

The dissimilar answers to these statements imply that although Israeli and American parents profess concerns about information privacy, the Americans are more engaged than the Israelis with concerns about the Web and how to deal with them. Additional divergences in the answers between the two groups suggest that when it also comes to responsibility for knowing about and acting on issues of Web privacy, Israeli parents depart from their U.S. counterparts in kind, not just degree. The first three statements reflect differences in what might be called a locus of privacy responsibility.

An overwhelming percentage of Americans agreed or strongly agreed that parents (first statement), government (second statement), and business (third statement) ought to be deeply involved in ensuring a Web safe from teens' disclosure of information. Israelis, by contrast, were much less invested in the responsibility of any of these entities. The differences are particularly stark if we look specifically at the percentage of parents who agreed strongly with them. Agreeing strongly implies a certain high concern about a policy issue; simply agreeing does not. We found that only 18% of Israeli parents, compared to 53% of the U.S. parents, agreed strongly that they expect businesses to help them with privacy-that they "look to see if a Web site has a privacy policy before answering any questions."

Moreover, while 88% of U.S. parents agreed strongly that "I should have a legal right to know everything that a Web site knows about me," only 43% of Israeli parents felt strongly about it. Similarly, 84% of U.S. versus 43% of Israeli parents agreed strongly that "teenagers should have to get their parent's consent before giving out information online." These differences in the locus of responsibility also translate into different practical conclusions that U.S. and Israeli parents draw from their sense of growing privacy exposure.

While a large proportion (47%) of Israeli parents compared to U.S. parents (10%) note that one of their children has "given out information he or she shouldn't to Web sites," only 4% of the Israelis (compared to 19% of the Americans) have installed filters to try to keep some control over the sites the teens can visit-even though one third of the Israelis (and 78% of Americans) say they have heard of filters.

This contrasting attitude toward a parent-initiated technological fix was even more striking when we explained the functions of filters and monitors to them and asked them, "If someone offered to help you put an internet filter or monitor on your computer for free, would you want the filter, the monitor or both?" Whereas 82% of the U.S. parents wanted one or both of these devices, only 43% of the Israelis did. This exploratory cross-cultural comparison has yielded patterns of difference and similarity that speak to both the cultural construction of privacy (and technology) and the political economy of globalization.

The responses by Israeli and American parents reveal very different perspectives on the Web's power and the locus of responsibility for controlling it. We noted that Israeli parents are much more skeptical than their U.S. counterparts about the transforming possibilities of the Web: They don't buy the hype about the Internet's advantages, and they don't accept the dystopic rhetoric about its dangers. In comparison, the answers of the American parents stand out as almost frantic over the impact of the Web (positive and negative) on their family lives.

Israeli and U.S. parents also don't see eye-to-eye when it comes to important aspects of domestic privacy and the Web. Far more American than Israeli parents say that their concern about Web privacy has increased since going online. Far more Americans say, too, that they are nervous about Web sites having information about them. Israelis also don't have nearly the commitment the Americans have to parental, governmental, or business solutions to Web privacy problems. They seem, instead, to feel that teens themselves should shoulder the burden of policing the borders of privacy.

Seeing these differences side-by-side underscores the constructed nature of the Web. To explain them, one can point to the traditional Israeli commitment to the collective over the private and to the continual sociopolitical tension that naturalizes and renders acceptable the violation of privacy by the government and military. The United States, by contrast, has created a hallowed position for individual privacy, though in ideal more than in practice. In the words of a New York Post commentator, "Americans don't like invasions of privacy, be it internet, health care or financial-related".

The disjunction between what Americans believe ought to be and what government and business often refuse to allow creates social tensions through which public advocacy groups try to force those institutions to create solutions. Government and business, by contrast, often reply by thrusting the responsibility for protecting privacy back to the hands of individuals and parents. That may lead to the tripartite solution that the survey uncovered among Americans, but not among Israelis.

This model highlighting local cultural constructions of the Web and Web privacy does not, however, fit all our data. We found that a clear majority of Israeli parents set aside their society's customary laxness over information privacy and agreed with American parents about the importance of not disclosing information to the Web. The great percentage of parents in both societies acknowledges being uncomfortable about themselves or their offspring confiding even rather superficial family information to marketers. Israelis' concerns mirror the American worries that they had seen and heard through a variety of print and electronic media channels, including a U.S.-centered Israeli version of the Web.

The similarities and differences imply that a complex dynamic is at work. The findings indicate that cross-cultural influences are intermingling with local cultural constructions to form a peculiar mix, neither American nor fully continuous with the Israeli "indigenous" tolerance for disclosure. We suggest that exposure to U.S. Web issues on Israeli media along with export-minded discussions of U.S. high-tech throughout society are leading Israeli parents to adopt Web-privacy worries that do not resonate with the nation's traditional privacy practices. Yet when it comes to the more profound step of actually acting on these issues-deciding if government or business or parents should take responsibility for preventing information disclosure-traditional Israeli perspectives on privacy do transfer to the Internet.

These explanations clearly need to be investigated further. What we have as a result of this research, though, are sharp indicators that a complex combination of forces is shaping Israeli responses to the Web and strong possibilities that some of those forces originate outside Israeli society. Comparative surveys across time can help us explore how much, how, and exactly why Israeli society is becoming more "American" in its attitudes toward the Web as Israeli business and media continue their Americentric scripts when it comes to high-technology. Comparative field research is also necessary to understand the actual ways that parents in the two societies approach the Web on the ground. How they are changed, by how much, and what resistance there is to "imported" views, are topics that require work both within and across portions of the global system.

The argument that some influences on Web attitudes reflect the global political economy even while other influences are local is a position that society-specific cultural accounts often ignore. Our framework and comparative survey findings suggest that, instead, it is a direction that needs to be explored. The challenge for researchers-particularly when it comes to countries outside the center of the world economy, but also in relation to those in it-is to continually relate people's attitudes, actions, and interactions to the national and global sociopolitical system. That, metaphorically and practically, is what "the Web" is really about.

VALID AND RELIABLE ASSESSMENT

Analyses of 10 raters' reasoning during think-aloud interviews provided evidence supporting a model of the fundamental processes involved in rating standards-based, nonprescriptive portfolios. Raters cycled iteratively among component processes and among subprocesses within them rather than following a linear sequence. This process model for portfolio rating provides a framework within which to conceptualize sound rater reasoning and to distinguish between acceptable variations and those that distort the meaning of scores. Score validity was threatened when raters omitted one of the major processes, evaluated portfolios without consideration of important criteria in the rating guide, or applied extraneous assessment criteria.

The 3 raters who exhibited these kinds of behaviours in their rating rationales generated ratings at a portfolio reading that were unacceptably inconsistent and unreliable. Furthermore, raters with identical patterns of problematic psychometric results were found to reason in substantially different ways, indicating that quantitative information alone is insufficient to detect and diagnose rating problems. Standards and the performance-based assessments that measure them are seen by many as essential to the systemic reform of education.

These assessments can make explicit for teachers, students, and the larger community what is important for students to accomplish, what serves as evidence of that accomplishment, and what level of student performance is valued. At the same time, in order for performance-based assessments to provide useful information, they must meet the same standards of validity and reliability as other educational and psychological assessments. Reports on the technical quality of performance assessments have been mixed, particularly with respect to portfolios.

For the most part, interrater agreement has been relied on to monitor the technical soundness of performance assessment ratings. Interrater agreement is not sufficient for establishing an assessment's validity, however. Raters may demonstrate high levels of agreement without their ratings being based on shared or appropriate judgments. Conversely, differences between ratings sometimes can represent more accurate and meaningful measurement than would absolute agreement-for example, a split between raters' judgments can reflect truly mixed performance on the part of an examinee. Measures of interrater reliability, then, do not necessarily indicate whether raters are making sound judgments and do not provide bases for improving technical quality.

In this chapter, we combine cognitive process with psychometric analyses to build empirical and theoretical foundations for establishing and monitoring the validity and reliability of portfolio assessments. Working within Messick framework of validity, we consider the role of raters' judgments in score validation. We postulate a process model of portfolio rater reasoning and define major threats to construct validity that can be introduced by important variations in reasoning. We then examine think-aloud protocols of raters' reasoning and inspect the relation between reasoning behaviours and psychometric measures of rating patterns, to evaluate the adequacy of our theoretical analysis.

CONSTRUCT VALIDITY AND RATER REASONING

"Validity is not a property of the test or assessment as such, but rather of the meaning of the test scores". The meaning of test scores is always a function of the assessment items or stimulus conditions, the examinees, and the context of an assessment. But in the case of performance assessments, scores are also a function of raters-the constructs being measured are determined in part by the process and content of raters' reasoning as they make their judgments. Discussions of validity criteria for performance assessments, therefore, need to extend beyond tasks and examinees to a consideration of raters' influence on score meaning.

One major aim of construct validation is to establish the extent to which assessments actually elicit the knowledge, skills, and other abilities they are intended to measure:

The substantive aspect (of construct validity) refers to theoretical rationales for the observed consistencies in test responses, including cognitive process models of task performance, along with empirical evidence that the theoretical processes are actually engaged by respondents in the assessment tasks.

But just as essential as models and studies of examinees' task performance are analyses of raters' judgments of that performance. Even if an assessment activity engages examinees in the desired aspects of a content domain and processes, the examinees' knowledge and abilities are reflected in scores only to the extent the raters bring to bear appropriate rating procedures and criteria-and raters do not always do so. Score validation must include, therefore, theories of the processes, strategies, and understandings underlying sound and appropriate raters' judgments and empirical evidence of the extent to which raters engage in the theoretical processes.

It is to these validation activities that we turn our attention in this work. In particular, we offer a theory of processes that might underlie rating of student portfolios and seek evidence that the process model captures essential features of raters' reasoning when they make rating judgments. We then attempt to identify and understand potential sources of invalidity by examining variations in raters' rating processes and application of assessment criteria. One of the theoretical and empirical questions explored here is how to distinguish the point at which variations become inappropriate, such that the assessment is not measuring desired constructs.

Thus far, cognitive processes underlying raters' reasoning have been described or modeled only in the context of essay rating. A schematic of these processes is provided, along with a depiction of basic processes that might be involved in portfolio rating, for purposes of comparison. According to Freedman and Calfee, a rater of an individual essay begins by attempting to read and interpret the text-a process of constructing an image of the text in long-term memory. As an image of the text is stored, the rater begins to evaluate the text image through a complex process that involves and is influenced by many factors, including the rater's understanding of the assessment criteria, prior experience, and background, and the situation in which the rater is working. Eventually, the rater decides what score to assign and articulates the rating.

This basic characterization was supported empirically and elaborated by Wolfe. These component processes could be executed as a linear sequence, but Freedman and Calfee speculated that the process may be recursive:

After articulating part of an evaluation, the rater continues to read and does not necessarily withhold evaluation until all the text has been read. Rather, as bits of text are comprehended, they are judged. Furthermore, the evaluation of one section of text may change as one comprehends a subsequent section of text.

Wolfe confirmed that some raters exhibit iterative processing and intermingle reading, evaluating, and articulating rating processes when judging essays. This iterative quality and the cyclical processing sequences that may result are represented by the various arrows leading in and out of the processes.

The fundamental processes involved in portfolio rating have yet to be described or documented. The task of evaluating multiple entries in a portfolio must elicit different processes than evaluation of a single text. However, different portfolio models would be expected to evoke different cognitive processes in the raters, so the portfolio and scoring model specified in a particular portfolio assessment system must be made explicit. In the system investigated in this chapter, no particular kinds of entries or standardized pieces of work were required in the portfolios. Rather, examinees were to select pieces that, when taken together, demonstrated their performance with respect to particular assessment dimensions.

Thus, portfolios were defined as collections of student work that were intended to be rated holistically along the dimensions-the individual entries in the portfolios were not to be rated separately from the collection as a whole. Given this definition, and by extension from the description of essay rating, we postulate that the process of rating portfolios of this kind can be thought of in terms of three essential component processes: (a) evaluating individual texts in the portfolio one at a time, (b) evaluating across texts in the portfolio, and (c) articulating a rating, weighing relative amounts or importance of evidence as needed.

The added complexity of rating portfolios over essays is depicted in several ways. First, whereas essay rating involves one individual text evaluation, the portfolio rating task as defined here involves not only multiple individual text evaluations but also evaluation across the collection of texts. That is, the portfolio raters must read and evaluate (but not rate) individual texts repeatedly in the course of evaluating a single portfolio. In addition, the portfolio raters have to describe and evaluate performance by reasoning across evidence in individual texts, a process that is not required in essay rating.

Second, whereas the essays in previous studies typically were generated in response to a standard prompt that was familiar to the raters, in this investigation portfolios did not contain required, prespecified pieces. Therefore, we would expect that raters would need to monitor the relevance and credibility of entries to determine whether to consider them as evidence. The closest that essay raters come to this kind of monitoring process is having to decide whether an essay is off-topic and therefore will not receive a rating.

Finally, as with essays, raters would be likely to cycle repeatedly through components of the portfolio rating process rather than performing them in a simple linear sequence. Because there are more component processes involved in rating portfolios than essays, these iterations could generate many variations in reasoning, but the variations would not necessarily represent threats to validity.

THREATS TO VALIDITY

In addition to exhibiting variations in the sequences in which they execute the processes, raters may differ in which processes they evoke and in what assessment criteria they bring to bear as they execute the processes. The validity of scores raters assign depends on the influence of any of these variations on score meaning. In this study, we examine raters' rating processes and application of assessment criteria to distinguish threats to validity from acceptable variations in reasoning.

Rating Processes

Threats to validity are introduced when raters (a) omit essential processes, (b) add extraneous and inappropriate processes, or (c) execute the processes in a sequence that adversely influences the meaning of the ratings they assign. In the portfolio system investigated here, the rating guides were written, and rater training designed, with the intention that the collection of evidence be evaluated as a whole with respect to particular assessment dimensions. Indeed, some criteria could be applied only by looking across multiple pieces of student work, for example, "communicates ... to a variety of audiences, for a variety of purposes, using a variety of genres", and "the work shows clear understanding of a variety of concepts and procedures".

A rater might depart from appropriate processing, for example, if she based her rating judgment only on the most recent piece looked at or the last one produced by the student. In such a case, the rater would have replaced the process of evaluation across texts with one involving selection and evaluation of an individual text, and the resulting rating would have a different meaning from one based on assessment of the collection of texts in the portfolio.

APPLICATION OF ASSESSMENT CRITERIA

There are two major threats to construct validity in assessments, both of which can be introduced in raters' application of assessment criteria:

In the one known as 'construct underrepresentation', the assessment is too narrow and fails to include important dimensions or facets of the construct. In the threat to validity known *as construct-*

irrelevant variance, the assessment is too broad, containing excess reliable variance associated with other distinct constructs.

Construct underrepresentation can be manifested as omission of assessment criteria or idiosyncratic weighing of criteria such that some aspects of performance do not receive sufficient evaluative attention. Construct-irrelevant variance can be introduced by raters' application of extraneous, irrelevant, or idiosyncratic criteria that are not part of the rating model they were trained to use. Distinguishing between construct-relevant and construct-irrelevant variance is often nontrivial but is especially difficult for performance assessments.

These complex assessments typically are intended to measure multiple underlying constructs that are not clearly separable or defined. Portfolios compound the difficulties by combining into one collection individual artifacts, each of which may tap multiple constructs. Raters can vary within and among themselves in how they weigh evidence in and across these artifacts. These variations, along with differences in rating processes and criteria, could introduce differences in the constructs being assessed. The greater these variations and differences, the more likely raters are to disagree with one another or to be erratic in assigning ratings.

REASONING AND RATING PATTERNS

Distributions of ratings and discrepancies between ratings are often monitored during performance assessment scoring sessions, but little is known about the relation between validity and rating patterns. Patterns that typically are treated as problematic include discrepancies that exceed some specified amount (e.g., 2 points on a 5-point scale); elevated or deflated rating averages or skewed rating distributions for an individual rater relative to the other raters; and other aberrant distributions indicating that raters are not using the full range of available scale points, such as when they avoid the extremes or the middle of the rating scale.

These patterns may occur for many different reasons, including differences in the constructs being assessed by different raters, in which processes are executed or which assessment criteria are applied, in the severity or leniency of raters, or in how raters interpret students' performances even if they are evaluating that evidence in relation to appropriate criteria. Different rater retraining interventions are indicated, depending on what kind of problem a rater exhibits. It is important to know which quantitative indicators can be relied on to detect substantive threats to validity in raters' judgments, as well as how to interpret the nature of the problems.

For these reasons, we also look at the relation between features of rater reasoning and psychometric measures of rating quality, in particular interrater reliability and intrarater consistency. To obtain authentic information about raters' reasoning and rating patterns during the rating of student assessment portfolios, we collected data in the context of a live portfolio reading session involving more than 80 raters rating hundreds of portfolios. At this reading, a sample of 10 verbal think-aloud protocols of the portfolio rating process was obtained from 10 raters as they each rated one portfolio. We analyzed both the raters' reasoning in the individual interviews and all of the ratings assigned by these same 10 raters in the larger reading. These analyses then allowed examination of the relation between reasoning and rating patterns.

This research was conducted as part of a project to develop a large-scale student portfolio assessment system for the state of California that would both support instructional improvement and provide trustworthy assessment information. At the time, California was engaged in an intensive, legislated redesign of its student assessment system. At the heart of the system under development-the California Learning Assessment System (CLAS)-was the belief that the primary purposes of assessment should be to improve public education and promote student learning.

To support high standards of student achievement, the state moved toward performance-based assessments, on demand as well as classroom based, that drew from, and were intended to influence, ongoing classroom instructional activities. As part of this effort, a team of Educational Testing

Service (ETS) researchers worked with California teachers and other advisors in 1992-1993 to develop a framework for the portfolio assessment system, and during the 1993-1994 school years, to develop and test preliminary versions of the portfolio materials and rating guides.

With instructional considerations at the forefront, the assessment portfolio had two key design features. First, the portfolios were to demonstrate student performance with respect to broad, essential dimensions of learning that specified the knowledge, skills, abilities, and habits of mind that student work should evidence in mathematics and language arts. Three dimensions of learning were defined for mathematics-Mathematical Content, Communicating Mathematics, and Putting Mathematics to Work-and two for language arts-Composing and Expressing Ideas, and Constructing Meaning.

These dimensions, based on the California curricular frameworks and national standards, constituted the content standards for the portfolios. The second key design feature was that no particular kinds of entries or standardized pieces of work were required for the portfolios. Rather, students, with help from their teachers, were to select those pieces of classroom work that, taken together, would provide strong evidence of their achievement with respect to the dimensions.

The instructional rationale for this standards-based, nonprescriptive assessment portfolio design was that it would help students and teachers focus on those qualities of performance that were most valued within the domain. They would need to think about which pieces of work actually did provide such evidence and what that evidence suggested with respect to a student's level of performance. Teachers might then ask themselves whether their instructional programs provided students sufficient opportunities to produce work that met the state's standards. Students might internalize the standards and use them to advance their own learning. In sum, this system aimed to engage teachers and students in active consideration of classroombased evidence with respect to public standards of performance. It put a premium on explicit criteria, classroom work, and the development of judgment by teachers and students of what these standards mean in the classroom.

In a 2-day portfolio reading in May 1994, teachers throughout California rated a sample of student portfolios in mathematics and language arts at Grades 4 and 8. Each rater assessed portfolios holistically along one of the dimensions at one grade level within a subject area, and each portfolio was rated twice along each dimension. A rater of Communicating Mathematics, Grade 4, for example, rated portfolios along that dimension and at that grade level only.

Portfolio rating guides were developed that specified criteria for distinguishing among four rating categories-Beginning, Developing, Accomplished, and Exemplary-and that also gave raters the opportunity to indicate that there was not enough evidence in the portfolio to judge a student's level of performance. The rating guides identified aspects within each dimension that were to be taken into account in rating the entire collection of student work along the dimension in question. Raters recorded their judgments on forms that included complete reproductions of the rating guides in order to help raters identify and keep track of which criteria best described qualities of students' performance.

A total of 84 raters rated portfolios during the reading. Approximately 75% of the raters were currently practicing teachers; close to 20% were school or district administrators, and the remainder were representatives of various educational projects and state or local departments of education. A sample of 10 individuals was randomly selected to be interviewed from the raters who were teachers, one from each of the 10 dimension and grade-level groups. Despite project efforts to obtain a rater pool that reflected the demographics of California's diverse student population, the pool of raters at the reading, and therefore the sample interviewed, reflected the more limited diversity in California's teacher population.

Training was conducted during the morning of both days of the reading. During each training session, benchmark portfolios were rated and discussed by each dimension and grade-level group. Raters were asked to read through the entire collection in each benchmark portfolio, look for specific evidence of achievement that was relevant to the dimension they were assessing, determine which description best fit the performance in the entire collection, and decide which of the four performance levels was most appropriate as an overall rating for the portfolio on that dimension.

During the last hour of the portfolio reading, three research staff members collected think-aloud protocols from the 10 raters. Each rater, along with the portfolio she or he happened to be given next in the reading session, was taken to a quiet room for an audiotaped interview. The rater was asked to assess the portfolio as he or she had been doing in the reading room, except for the additional instruction to think out loud while deciding how to rate the portfolio. After a rating was decided on for the portfolio, the interviewer asked for a summary of the rater's reasons for the ultimate portfolio rating, as well as elaboration or clarification of the rater's earlier comments as needed.

The think-aloud interviews, which lasted between 20 and 40 min, yielded 10 transcripts of reasoning during the rating process, for 10 different raters and 10 different portfolios. The portfolios and the rating forms completed by the raters during the interviews were photocopied for reference during the analysis.

Close to 600 fourth- and eighth-grade portfolios were submitted by 26 teachers in 15 schools across the state of California. A sample of the portfolios to be assessed in the reading was randomly selected, balancing only for gender. At the reading, 217 portfolios received two ratings on each dimension (i.e., excluding those without enough evidence to judge), for a data set of over 1,000 ratings. We included in these analyses only a subset of these ratings-those assigned on 177 portfolios by the 10 raters from whom think-aloud protocols were collected, along with the second ratings assigned by other raters who evaluated portfolios in common with these 10 raters, a total of 354 ratings.

Our first analytic task was to characterize raters' reasoning behaviours in the think-aloud interviews to evaluate the process model. We then examined the protocols for evidence of threats to validity in raters' processes and application of assessment criteria. Finally, we examined the relation between the quality of rater reasoning and two psychometric indicators of their performance as raters-interrater reliability and intrarater consistency.

Each protocol was transcribed and separated into conceptually distinct statements or phrases. A hermeneutic, iterative approach was used to classify raters' rating behaviours with respect to the processes specified in the model. More specifically, one of the authors and a colleague each read and annotated the transcripts to identify raters' reasoning behaviours. Any differences of opinion were discussed and used to clarify our understandings until agreement was reached about the behaviours exhibited in the transcripts.

The transcripts were coded with respect to the appropriateness of raters' rating processes-whether raters evaluated portfolios in accordance with the overall rating procedure that they were trained to use and therefore with the proposed process model; and application of assessment criteria-whether raters applied criteria that were consistent with an appropriate rating guide and considered all major aspects of the assessment dimensions.

All of the raters' comments were examined closely and each behaviour was noted whenever it was observed at all-that is, whether the behaviour appeared once or throughout an entire segment of the transcript, it was coded as present. We applied these codes to the entire interview protocol, noting whether behaviours indicative of a code were present or not, regardless of the frequency of those behaviours. This approach was used because the portfolios varied in length and other characteristics and therefore afforded different opportunities for raters to exhibit certain behaviours.

The analysis also included an examination of the relation between reasoning behaviours during the think-aloud session for each of the 10 raters interviewed and psychometric indicators of their performance as raters during the portfolio reading. Rating performance was measured in two ways-by examining interrater agreement and intrarater consistency. Interrater agreement is a simple indication of congruence between the ratings assigned by a rater and those assigned by other raters in her or his dimension and grade-level group, on the same portfolios.

The proportion of exact agreement for each rater interviewed was calculated as the ratio of the number of ratings that were exactly the same as a second rater's rating to the total number of portfolios rated in common with other raters.

Intrarater consistency is a measure of the extent to which the ratings assigned by an individual conform to what would be expected, and are internally consistent, based on some model of performance. Rater inconsistency can manifest itself in several ways. In comparison with the rating patterns of other more consistent raters, the inconsistent rater does not use the rating scales in the same way for all students and appears unable to maintain his or her personal level of severity when rating students.

The rater may give a number of ratings that are unexpectedly high or unexpectedly low, taking into account the rater's overall level of seventy and the ratings given by the other raters who rated those same students. When compared with other raters, a rater may use certain points disproportionately often, or one or more raters may use the rating scale in a way that is clearly idiosyncratic. Although a rater who is internally inconsistent may be expected to exhibit low levels of interrater agreement, the relation between these measures, and between these psychometric indicators of rating performance and rater reasoning, has not been examined.

Measures of intrarater consistency were obtained for each rater in the sample using Facets, a computer program that performs many-faceted Rasch modeling. The Facets program constructs a model of the measurement situation that takes into account various sources of measurement error. The measurement model employed by Facets makes predictions as to how a given rater will rate a given student, taking into account not only how that rater has rated other students of similar levels of ability but also the ratings that other raters gave that student.

The model examines the rater's ratings for a student to determine to what extent each rating is consistent with the general pattern of ratings observed for that student. The model then compares the observed values to the expected values that are determined by the measurement model and computes residuals that reflect the difference between what was observed and what was expected. The fit indices that Facets produces provide summary measures of the extent to which the rater's ratings are (or are not) in accord with the predictions of the measurement model.

An inconsistent rater is one who has a great amount of unmodeled variation in his or her ratings. The variation in that rater's ratings cannot adequately be explained by the measurement model employed. The Facets program produces two statistics for each rater that indicate that rater's intrarater consistency, or the degree to which each rater is internally consistent: (a) the outlier-sensitive fit statistic, referred to hereafter as "mean-square outfit"; and (b) the information-weighted mean-square fit statistic, referred to hereafter as "mean-square infit." "Outfit" statistics are heavily influenced by the occasional outlying, off-target and highly unexpected rating.

An alternative is to weigh residuals by the information they contain so that the fit statistics are information weighted or "infits" that are sensitive to patterns of many small differences between expected and observed ratings. Because each rater rated only one learning dimension at one grade level, 10 separate Facets analyses had to be performed, one for the rating data from each dimension at each grade level. These analyses were run for groups as small as five, and hence must be interpreted with caution.

In this section, we describe and illustrate the nature of raters' rating processes through examples of what raters said in the think-aloud interviews. We then identify threats to the validity of ratings that were introduced by variations in the rating processes and assessment criteria raters brought to bear. We conclude by examining the relation between raters' reasoning during the think-aloud interviews and psychometric measures of the reliability and consistency with which they assigned ratings during the portfolio reading.

This part of the results is organized around the major rating processes in the model-evaluating individual texts, evaluating across text images, and articulating a rating. We begin by summarizing raters' reasoning behaviours in the think-aloud interviews with respect to the processes in the model and then provide illustrative examples of these behaviours. Behaviours that were consistent with every component process were exhibited by almost all of the raters.

The only exceptions were two cases in which no comments were made that corresponded to monitoring admissibility, and one rater who did not rate the portfolio on the basis of evaluation across entries. In the following sections we characterize rating processes in rich detail using quotes from the interviews. These descriptions are intended to provide the reader with an understanding of typical reasoning behaviours.

Bibliography

Adburgham, Alison. *Women in Print. Writing Women and Women's Magazines from Restoration to the Accession of Victoria.* London: Allen & Unwin, 1972.

Arnold, Ethel M. *Literature for Ladies, 1830-1930.* Manhattan: K.S.A.C. Press, 1930.

Barrell, Joan. *The Business of Women's Magazines.* 2nd ed. London: Kogan Page, 1988.

Beetham, Margaret. *Victorian Women's Magazines : An Anthology.* Manchester: Manchester University Press, 2001.

Boston Women's Health Book Collective. *Our Bodies Ourselves.* New York: Simon & Schuster, 1976.

Braithwaite, Brian. *The Business of Women's Magazines: The Agonies and the Ecstasies.* London: Associated Business Press, 1979.

Braithwaite, Brian. *Women's Magazines: The First 300 Years.* London: Peter Owen, 1995.

Brody, Michal, ed. *Are We There Yet? A Continuing History of Lavender Woman.* Iowa City; Aunt Lute Company, 1985.

Burman, Barbara, ed. *The Culture of Sewing: Gender, Consumption and Homedressmaking (Dress, Body, Culture).* Oxford: Berg, 1999.

Coakley, Mary Lewis. *1907-Sex, Sisterhood, and Self-Delusion: What Happened to Women's Magazines?* New Rochelle: Arlington House, c. 1979.

Dancyger, Irene. *A World of Women. An Illustrated History*

of Women's Magazines. Dublin: Gill and Macmillian, 1978.

Danky, James P., ed. *Women's Periodicals and Newspapers from the 18th Century to 1981: A Union List of the Holdings of Madison, Wisconsin Libraries.* Boston: GK Hall, 1982.

Doughan, David, and Denise Sanchez. *Feminist Periodicals, 1855-1984: An Annotated Critical Bibliography of British, Irish, Commonwealth and International Titles.* Brighton: Harvester, 1987.

Eskridge, Melissa J. *How the Psychology of Women Is Presented in Women's Magazines,* 1986.

Ferguson, Marjorie. *Forever Feminine: Women's Magazines and the Cult of Femininity.* London: Heinemann, 1983.

Friedan, Betty. *The Feminine Mystique.* New York: Dell Publishing Co., Inc., 1963.

Gough-Yates, Ann. *Understanding Women's Magazines: Publishing, Markets and Readership.* London: Routledge, 2003.

Grimstad, Kirsten and Susan Rennie, eds. *The New Woman's Survival Catalog.* New York: Berkley Publishing Corporation, 1973.

Hermes, Joke. *Reading Women's Magazines: An Analysis of Everyday Media Use.* Cambridge: Polity Press, 1995.

Hoffmann, Phyllis P. *Women's Magazines.* 1983.

Incantalupo, Patricia. *The Portrayal of Women in Sport Advertising in Two Women's Fitness Magazines,* 1992.

Johnson, Judy M, ed. *Spot Illustrations from Women's Magazines of the Teens and Twenties: 828 Cuts of Women, Family, Home, Garden, Etc.* New York: Dover Publications, 1989.

Mann, Robert S. "Women and the Newspaper." *The University of Missouri Bulletin,* no. 2640.

Millum, Trevor. *Images of Woman: Advertising in Women's Magazines.* London: Chatto & Windus, 1975.

Ramet, Adèle. *Creating a Twist in the Tale: How to Write Winning Short Stories for Women's Magazines.* Plymouth: How To Books, 1996.

Shevelow, Kathryn. *Women and Print Culture: The Construction of Femininity in the Early Periodical.* London: Routledge, 1989.

Sievers, Sharon L. *Flowers in Salt: The Beginnings of Feminist Consciousness in Modern Japan.* Stanford: Stanford University Press, 1983.

Waller, Jane, and Michael Vaughan-Rees. *Women in Wartime; the Role of Women's Magazines 1939-1945.* London: Macdonald Optima, 1987.

White, Cynthia L. "Growth between the Wars: 1920-1938." In *Women's Magazines 1693-1968.* London: Michael Joseph Ltd, 1970.

White, Cynthia L. *Women's Magazines 1693-1968.* London: Michael Joseph Ltd, 1970.

Winship, Janice. *Advertising in Women's Magazines, 1956-74.* Birmingham: Centre for Contemporary Cultural Studies, University of Birmingham, 1980.

Winship, Janice. *Inside Women's Magazines.* New York: Pandora, 1987.

Yackey, Lena Millicent. *Contributions of Women's Magazines to Homemaking Problems on Food.* New York, 1930.

Index